STREET TALK

Compiled by Jeffrey Miller

Edited By Graham Nown

Ward Lock Limited · London

First published in Great Britain in 1986
by Ward Lock Limited, 8 Clifford Street,
London W1X 1RB, an Egmont Company

Designed by Melissa Orrom
Text filmset in Cheltenham Light
by Foremost Typesetting Ltd, London SE1
Printed and bound in Italy
by Canale

British Library Cataloguing in Publication Data

Miller, Jeffrey
Street talk: a Coronation Street
dictionary.
1. Coronation Street (Television program)
—— Dictionaries
I. Title II. Nown, Graham
791.45′72′0321 PN1992.77.C6/

ISBN 0-7063-6514-3

PUBLISHER'S ACKNOWLEDGMENTS

Grateful thanks to Granada Television, especially *Coronation Street* executive producer, Bill Podmore, for his help and advice; archivist Eric Rosser, the Street's memory man; and scriptwriter and elder statesman H.V. Kershaw, who has shaped so many *Coronation Street* milestones.
Thanks also to Ken Howarth of the North West Sound Archive, and Dr Peter Wright of Salford University.

COMPILER'S ACKNOWLEDGMENTS

Special mention must be made of the late Eric Partridge, whose scholarship, like that of Dr Johnson before him, was unaided, and unimpeded, by academic tenure; E.C. Dann, assistant editor of *The New Oxford Dictionary,* who patiently answered many questions that must often have seemed lunatic; and H.V. Kershaw, eminent Mancunian and a father of *Coronation Street.*

Thanks also to my 'eastern' friend Chris Bayliss for his advice on Gordon Bennett and other sticky etymological wickets; to Glenn Witmer, Bob Daley, Polly Manguel, and Kim Obrist of CBC Enterprises for their enthusiasm, friendship, and multifarious assistance; to Ward Lock, Eric Rosser, and Graham Nown for their hard work against time; to Cathy Ellis, for access to her Street files; and to Ed O'Dacre and Mary Doyle of the Toronto *Globe and Mail* for taking an early interest in the project.

Primary sources are cited below. Their publishers are Oxford University (OED), Routledge and Kegan Paul (Partridge), Hodder and Stoughton (Phythian), and Macmillan (Schur). The story under **wellies** about the Duke of Wellington and Queen Victoria is reported in Robert Hendrickson's *Human Words,* Chilton, 1972.

A small portion of this book appeared, in a very different form, in the Toronto *Globe and Mail.*

PRIMARY SOURCES

Dann — E.C. Dann (by correspondence with author), *New Oxford English Dictionary*

OED — *The Oxford English Dictionary* and its supplements, 1928-1986

Partridge — Eric Partridge, *A Dictionary of Slang and Unconventional Usage,* 1960

Phythian — B.A. Phythian, *Concise Dictionary of English Slang and Colloquialisms,* 1976

Schur — Norman W. Schur, *British Self-Taught: With Comments in American,* 1973

Where a word or phrase in a definition is in **bold face,** that word or phrase has a separate entry of its own.

FOREWORD

NOW YOU'RE TALKING!

Street talk – the everyday language of *Coronation Street* for the past twenty-six years – is in some ways no different from any other talk. English people understand it, most of it anyway, even if they don't say 'ecky thump!' or own an outdoor 'cludgy'.

What is perhaps unique about Britain's longest-running TV drama series is that it keeps alive a heritage of spoken English which, after centuries of common usage, is slowly disappearing. And it is kept alive not for any altruistic reasons, but because in vast untamed areas of Britain north of Birmingham it is simply the way ordinary people speak.

Some of it is rich in visual imagery: people 'thrutch' their way to the front of queues; lumbering Stan Ogden was 'a great lummock' when he used to get under Hilda's feet; and who can deny that Mavis Riley always looks 'gobsmacked'.

There is, too, a bucketful of comforting wisdom as we stumble through life's minefield together: 'start as you mean to go on', and 'never mind chuck, worse things happen at sea'. How different things might be if we took heed and never went out without a clean hanky, ensured we always had 'proper dinners' and believed in the restorative properties of 'a good lie down and a nice cup of tea'.

Some of the words and phrases in *Street Talk* have been used since the Middle Ages, others derive from the Victorian underworld, or started life in the mills and mines of the industrial revolution. A few are the very warp and weft of our language. Those who say ''em' instead of 'them', for instance, may take comfort from the fact that ''em' was around for centuries before 'them' was imported from Scandinavia. On the other hand, they probably couldn't give a monkey's. Many of the words and phrases in *Street Talk* will be regarded as commonplace by English readers but, taken together, they present an interesting picture of the expressions most commonly used on Britain's most consistently popular TV programme.

Jeffrey Miller, who compiled them, is a brave man indeed. He conceived the book to help millions of North Americans who are addicted to the Street, but mystified by 'mushy peas' and what Bet means when she is 'chuffed to little mint balls'. Once under way he found himself navigating deep waters. Miller is an American who moved to Canada and soon became hooked himself on *Coronation Street*, which has been screened there daily. Wrestling with unfamiliar expressions, such as 'will I eck as like!' or 'dead common', proved a task which expanded into lengthy correspondence with the bemused staff of the *Oxford English Dictionary*.

Soap operas, by their very nature, are supposed to reflect the life of our times. The Street, however, has always doggedly referred to itself as a 'folk-opera' and, like most folk, changes only by degrees. Despite new blood and current affairs bandied in the Rovers, attitudes and values, like those of real life, are rooted somewhere in the past. The specific year varies from character to character. For some there is a feeling it was when boys were christened Frank and Roy, and girls called Nellie or

Florrie wore ribbons in their hair. They had holidays at Butlins, and read the *Beano*. Mum and Dad took the *Mirror*, and wondered if they should write to Horace Bachelor in Keynsham, Bristol. Others were raised on package flights to Benidorm, collected Italian soccer cards and grew up to become *Sun* readers.

Like values, the things we say and the way we say them do not change quickly. The language of *Coronation Street* has moved, quite rightly, at a sedate pace. Street talk, overheard in Alf's Mini Market, or above the whine of Mike Baldwin's sewing machines, is quite unlike anything in other British soaps. There is a mixture of northernisms, historical slang, and the everyday words and phrases which are the currency of working-class life. There is no social message in the Street, no pseudo rhyming-slang – simply the voice of common people (dead common, some of them). Ribald, wryly humorous and preoccupied with the small-print of daily life in a quirkily British way, there is something of all of us in *Coronation Street*, irrespective of social background, which is probably why it raises such a smile.

Anyone fortunate enough to have relished gobstoppers, or watched lemonade crystals spooned from a jar with all the solemnity of gold dust, will have grown up on Coronation Street. They will have run errands to the corner shop, been chased by Percy Sugden and read their comics walking back from the Kabin. *Coronation Street* is as familiar as fish and chips. It preserves a way of life which lingers in the north of England, and in the memory of millions of viewers. The things they say have a bluntness, wit, and refreshing common sense which gives a much-needed lift to our sophisticated times.

Aside from the drama, and there is plenty of that, Street talk is one reason why millions never miss Britain's best-loved soap. It is often earthy, occasionally erudite and, most importantly, always entertaining. After all, as they say down Weatherfield way, you're a long time dead.

Graham Nown

INTRODUCTION

CONFESSIONS OF A CLOSET STREETIE

I don't want to scare anyone away, but this book is more serious than it might look.

It all started with guilt – shame, even – that I felt over a secret and profound addiction, an addiction not just to a television show, but to that bane of sensibility, a *soap opera*. Worse, this soap opera formed an especially insidious habit because in Toronto, my hometown, it was broadcast not the traditional five, but *six* days a week, with an extra half-hour on 'the Lord's day'.

Oh, I had my excuses. By three o'clock of an afternoon, I needed a chance to empty my mind over tea. Or, in my authorial solitude, it was salutary to have cathode-ray friends, especially during the merciless, snowbinding Canadian winter. Then, too, the soap was British and therefore educational, or at least it gave me a glimpse of cultural life across the pond, however distorted by its boob tube context. Best of all, Sir John Betjeman was famously a fan of the show, and *he* was a great poet.

I needed to believe what my heart already felt – that *Coronation Street* wasn't just more escapist television nonsense. I was already genuinely curious about the colorful colloquial language used so skilfully by the writers and actors. And so I wasn't prevaricating when, on the further excuse of celebrating the Street's twenty-fifth anniversary, I sold an article to the Toronto *Globe and Mail* which said:

It is often remarked, especially during the birthday celebrations, that *Coronation Street's* focus on the ordinary is what makes it extra-ordinary, particularly when the show is compared to American soap operas. Its stories are determinedly unglamorous, empathizing (not without condescension, perhaps) with the ordinary working stiff and traditional working-class values. Granada (Granada Television, the producers of *Coronation Street*) delights in quoting a typical criticism of the program's first episodes, from the *Daily Mirror*: The program is doomed from the outset – with its signature tune and grim scenes of a row of terraced houses and smoking chimneys . . .'

But the show's naturalistic grit is only half the appeal, especially to those of us otherwise repelled by most of television. It may be overstating the case to describe *Coronation Street* as Shakespearean (one thinks of Falstaff and Bottom and Mistress Quickly . . .), but certainly its manner of presentation – the writing, the show's narrative style, and especially its depiction of a colorful north-country dialect and banter – lend it a narrative and intellectual depth that are more common on the stage than TV. Sir John Betjeman, the famous British poet – and also President for Life of the British League for Hilda Ogden – once compared *Coronation Street* to Dickens's *Pickwick Papers*. 'Mondays and Wednesdays I live for them. Thank God, half past seven tonight and I shall be in Paradise.'

The language – the writing coupled with the superior acting – is all. Work, for instance, the prime preoccupation of the barely pecunious Weatherfieldians, is never just 'work'; it is always paid proper onomatopoeic respect for its ability to grind down the working person (on the Street, the 'two-career family' is no new liberation). It is always 'hard graft', or, in Hilda Ogden's case as charwoman, 'skivvying', derived from 'slaveying', working as a female slave.

After a long day of such hard graft, Weatherfieldians might wander into the Rovers Return, the corner pub that is the center of the action on the Street, and tell anyone who will listen that they're 'knackered', not just tired, but altogether used up, a knacker orginally having been an old and worn-out horse. And occasionally, when someone on the Street can't even raise the 'brass' to buy a pint, life's greatest, or only, consolation is a nice hot 'cuppa'. By now ('be now'), Bet Lynch, for years barmaid and now manager at the Rovers Return, has become famous for something like, 'Eee, Betty, luv, I could murder a cuppa' – a cuppa tea, of course.

Now my habit boasted a rationale that made me a cathode-ray Samuel Johnson. And I had even realized some professional profit out of it, albeit the journalist's usual niggling one.

I had found a really good excuse to watch *Coronation Street* six days a week, and the excuse grew into a sort of obsession in its own right. Now as I watched, I lay in wait for the very best sources of Street vernacular – charwoman Hilda Ogden, of course, and the Duckworths – especially loudmouth Vera, notoriously difficult for North Americans to understand, particularly during those not unusual occasions when she was steamed up and 'skrikering'. More surprisingly, there was the plumply respectable and avuncular grocer and town councillor, Alf Roberts, sure to have the quaintest expressions at hand – 'footling little barmcake orders', 'go and put your slap on', 'same to you with knobs on it'.

The *Globe* article had given me an excuse to research the expressions I picked up, and to discover that while the exigencies of drama required that the actors on *Coronation Street* be especially articulate, the vernacular was a legitimate, if slightly literary, one. I had already begun to make note of the broader linguistic characteristics of Street-talk – the tendency evidently general in certain sectors of British society to use *us* for *me* or *my* or *our* and the pronunciation of 'air' as 'ur', so that, when combined with a general inclination not to overwork the tongue 'I want Clare out of my hair', could come out 'A wan Clur outta me ur'. In the general spider's tangle of pronunciation and grammar, syntax was caught, kill't and struggled into a life beyond, a simple 'Give me that' transubstantiated into 'Give us that there', pronounced 'Giviss a thur'. When not dispensed with altogether, t's and the diphthong th were elided in a way, as I was sure would surprise the not-very-francophile Weatherfieldians, that was *très français* – 'Come up't th'office'. Indeed, dispensing with t's did not necessarily mean dropping them: often they were turned into r's: 'Ger away with your bother!' 'Whar 'appened 'ere?' H's, too, got Frenchified, as they had long before Eliza Dolittle – ''oy! You 'ave to come to us 'ouse at 'alf past six' – and verb and subject were routinely mismatched in elegant earthiness, deliberate misuse of the subjunctive: 'He were in a funny mood.' 'She hadn't laughed so hard since Adam were a lad!'

As my collection of words and phrases grew into a vocabulary, a psychology emerged with it, although whether it is the psychology of Lancashire and Greater Manchester or the psychology of the writers of *Coronation Street* I am not sure. The teeming sub-glossary of idioms for abandonment – scarper, skive, do a bunk, do a flit, do a runner, sling your hook, slope off . . . – attested that *some* group across the pond either was nonchalantly terrible about social responsibility or, more likely, terribly worried about it. I noticed, as well, a facility with mild abuse, oath-making, and imprecation, an inventiveness I heartily wished North Americans had the pride and imagination to emulate. Over here, I'm afraid, it's always the same half-dozen banalities invoking sex, anatomy, or excretion in situations that have nothing to do with biology, often by people who should have more to say for themselves. I suppose there are North American equivalents for the colorful *daft aper, daft pie-can, great nana, barmpot,* and *nutter.* But *Flaming Nora, Gordon Bennett,* and *Blimey O'Reilly* have sneaked into my vocabulary as friends with honest, righteous, working-class faces, heart-felt but never scandalizing oaths.

All of which is to say that doing this book has been enormous fun – too much fun for the sort of bloke who feels guilty about watching television. Beetle-browed effort has therefore been expended to provide accurate, sometimes (dare I say) scholarly, definitions and word histories. Occasionally, of course, because of the usual time-constraints in publishing, this has not been possible. And inevitably, where information is scant or uncertain, our guesses at an etymology may not be as good as those of some of our readers. (I say 'our' because not only my publishers, but Granada Television as well as Messrs. Graham Nown and Eric Rosser have been instrumental to this project, albeit from across the pond, and thereby with the complications such long-distance international communication entails!) In any event, critics will kindly keep in mind that although I am a keen student of language, I am not a Briton but an expatriate American living in Canada. (Anyone who writes about language quickly learns to take to heart a motto of the great lexicographer Eric Partridge, whose work was instrumental to this book: 'He who never makes mistakes makes nothing.') I would indeed love to hear from readers who know better than I (or even just think they do), who may write me care of Street-talk, CBC Enterprises, Box 500, Postal Station A, Toronto, Ontario, Canada M5W 1E6.

I would especially like to know who Nora is and why the poor woman so often bursts into flames – see **flaming nora,** page 40. This is, after all, a very *serious* book.

Jeffrey Miller
Toronto. June, 1986

Note: this book is a compendium of idiomatic British English, mostly Lancashire English as, and only as, that language is portrayed in the scripts of *Coronation Street.* Some more generally British idioms heard on the series are included if they would not necessarily be familiar to the general (often non-British) reader.

‘If you’ve never been to Weatherfield, you’ve never lived . . .’

abide: tolerate. 'Vera! You know I can't abide rice pudding.'
acid, acid drops: sarcastic, scathing, as in, 'What's wrong with her – she's full of acid drops.' Alarmingly sour sweets called acid drops were once sold in Florrie Lindley's corner shop. At their most potent they contract the cheeks and pucker the lips, giving an impression of ill-humour. *To come the acid* is to speak sarcastically or scathingly.
Adam's ale: water. Also known as 'corporation pop'.
afters: dessert, second course, as in, 'There's pineapple chunks and condensed milk for afters'. Despite Annie Walker's gourmet aspirations, few have achieved Hilda Ogden's command of afters. For her pearl wedding anniversary in 1973, she decided upon eggs in aspic. When a search for aspic in the corner shop proved fruitless, Hilda, undeterred, purchased a lemon jelly from the Co-op. Her taste for such exotica was acquired when cleaning for Dr and Mrs Lowther, who live in Oakfield – a high-class area just outside Weatherfield known witheringly as 'the debtors' retreat'. Mrs Lowther allowed Hilda to take home the left-overs from her 'afternoons'.
aggro: aggravation, in the jargon sense of annoyances or problems. Both Brian Tilsley and Alan Howard, proprietors of a garage, had 'a lot of aggro' from customers dissatisfied with car repairs.
alicker: vinegar. Possibly from *alec,* a pickling sauce.
all done up and dusted: finished, completed. Hilda – the doyenne of the duster – usually says, 'I'm done now, Mr Baldwin.'
all over bar the shouting: signifies the end of something, except for the talking and argument, which will change nothing. Probably of sporting origin.
all sorted: from 'all sorted out' – all set up and ready to go. Commonly heard amidst preparations for a week in Blackpool. The suitcases are packed, the *charabanc* is waiting – 'Are we all sorted, chuck?'
all sorts: all kinds of people, things or activities. Often said pejoratively, as in, 'You get all sorts in a neighbourhood like that'. Old ladies use it darkly, referring to the Street's rougher diamonds: 'Those folk get up to all sorts.' (i.e., are always involved in unconventional, illegal or annoying behaviour). Licorice allsorts, a confectionery assortment invariably containing some you like and others you loathe, were made just over the Pennines from Weatherfield.
allus: always, in a pronunciation which suggests illiteracy. Dennis Tanner, the black sheep of the Street, used it frequently: 'Gerroff Mam, you're allus pickin' on me!' Elsie Tanner, for her part, was, according to Ena Sharples, 'allus dressed up like a dog's dinner' (see **mutton dressed as lamb**).
alright: you're (he's, she's etc.) alright. Reassurance to those who apologize or worry about their behaviour. When Mike Baldwin only has a tenner to pay for his

scotch, Bet Lynch assures him: 'You're alright, cock – I've plenty of change.' Also a mild sexual connotation. One male may dig another in the ribs at the sight of an attractive girl and say: 'She's a bit of alright.' Or, as romeo Terry Duckworth might remark to Curly Watts: 'You'll be alright there, mate', knowing full well that he does not stand a chance.
and all: more commonly *an'all*, meaning also. 'I could wring Percy Sugden's neck at times.' 'Yeah, me an'all.'
and the rest: an expression of dry sarcasm at least 125 years old which suggests, 'As long as you're telling tales, why are you leaving anything out?' When Phyllis Pearce, no spring chicken, was celebrating her birthday, someone asked if she was 21. 'And the rest', she replied. The American equivalent is the heavily sceptical 'Sure thing!'
'anky: handkerchief. 'Taking a clean 'anky' is essential when leaving the house for a special occasion. 'Ankies are used in Weatherfield to blow **conks** and for moistening with spittle to wipe small children's faces in public. There is a certain social stigma attached to taking out a dirty 'anky, and people go to great lengths to keep them clean. Children who eat doughnuts on buses are reprimanded by mothers: 'I told you not to wipe that jam on your 'anky – wipe it on the seat!'
anyroad: anyway, anyhow (see **road**). Occasionally *anyroad up*.
aper: someone who acts, or says something, foolish. Ivy Tilsley usually prefixes it with 'daft'. A linguistic telescoping of ha'porth, or half-penny's worth, denoting less than intellectual full-measure, or perhaps from *ape*. Someone who is a *daft aper* might well not have *all his chairs at home*, or be 'as thick as a navvy's boot-lace'.

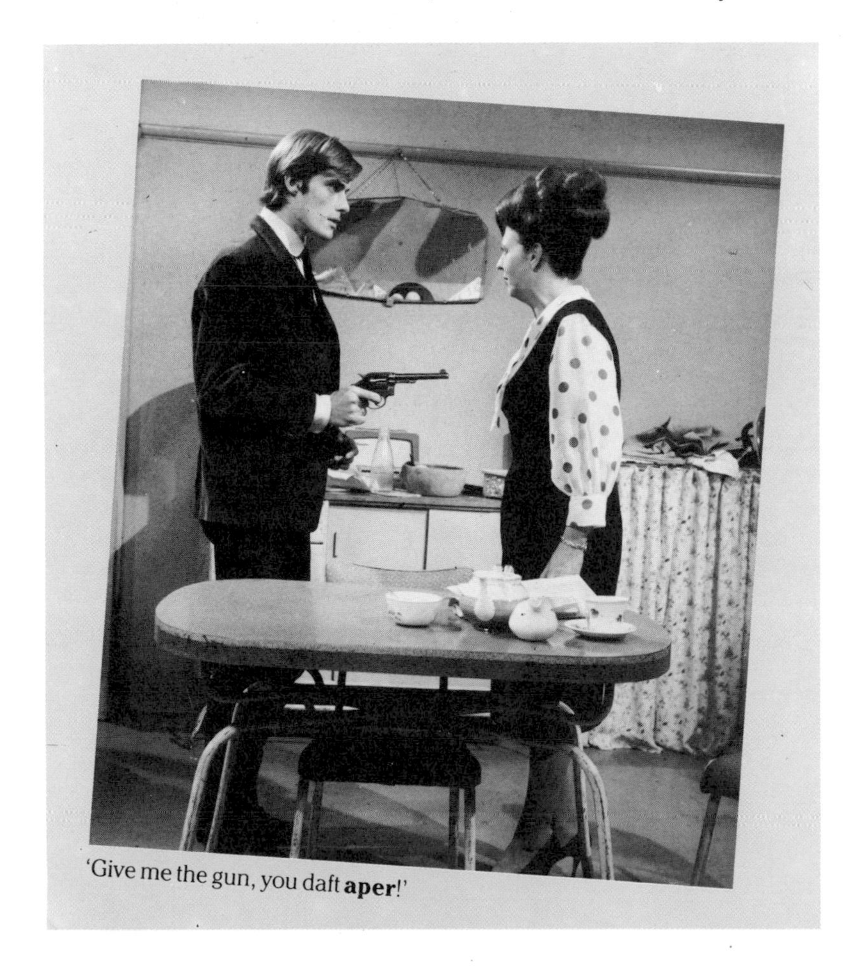

'Give me the gun, you daft **aper**!'

'appen: perhaps. A phrase preceded by happen, or 'appen, is archetypal Lancashire. 'Albert Tatlock has promised drinks all-round in the Rovers.' 'Aye, and 'appen pigs might fly.'
argue the toss: dispute vigorously. Derived, perhaps, from pitch and toss, an illegal street-corner gambling game prevalent in Weatherfield and the north of England during the Depression. *Coronation Street* residents frequently argue the toss. Ena Sharples and Albert Tatlock were past masters of the art.
argy-bargy (aŕjee-baŕjee): nagging argument or contrariness, one step more vociferous and nearer to violence than **argue the toss**. Len Fairclough was the instigator of many classic Street argy-bargies, which often resulted in an exchange

An **argy-bargy.**

of blows. The old form of the expression was *argal-bargal*, *argal* being a corruption of 'ergo'. Thus a clown in *Hamlet* concludes a pseudo-philosophical argument with, 'Argal, he that is not guilty of his own death shortens not his own life.'
article: when speaking of people, used in the sense of 'thing', as in the mild 'You cheeky article!' Also used to discuss a stranger's character in his absence: 'He were a right funny article' – he was an extremely peculiar individual. *Make an article of someone:* make a (contemptible) spectacle of someone. One definition of article given by Partridge is 'a woman exported to the Argentine to become a prostitute'.
as happy as Larry: a state of satisfaction, ranging from euphoric to contented. Possibly from the Australian *larrikin,* a young street rowdy, but the expression is less common in *Coronation Street* nowadays than 'as happy as a pig in muck'. 'Grinning like a butcher's dog' conveys the same emotional state.
as if!: indicates scepticism at a rumour or remark. 'They say Mike Baldwin's giving all the girls a Christmas bonus.' 'As if!'
aught: see **owt** and **summat**.

babby: baby, in the East Lancashire pronunciation favoured by Ivy Tilsley. See **childer**.
back-end: autumn. From horse-racing (the end of the season).
back-hander: in *Coronation Street,* an unexpected blow with the back of the hand. Elsewhere the expression is common slang for a bribe.

Gail, Brian and **babby**.

backyard: small enclosed courtyard behind terraced house. *Coronation Street* backyards were originally all equipped with standard **cludgy** a **midden** to dispose of material from the cludgy, a back gate painted with cricket stumps, a clothes line, and several loose bricks to balance on while gossiping over the wall. Some houses, when modernized, used the old kitchen sink, or **slopstone**, as backyard flower-troughs. The Ogdens' backyard has been the base for many doomed business ventures, including the stabling of a donkey called Dolores – until Weatherfield's public health inspector ordered its removal because the smell offended Annie Walker. In the U.S. and Canada, backyard is the equivalent of back garden.
bad 'un: that is, a bad one. Disreputable person, ruffian, a **wrong 'un**, *a bad lot.* Then there are those who are not *bad 'uns,* but 'the devil follows them around'. Ena Sharples was fond of such gothic judgements. *In extremis*, she referred to one

'You see, Jerry, there are **good 'uns** and **bad 'uns** in this life.'

particular bad 'un as having 'a heart as black as the devil's knitting bag'.
bagging: worker's packed lunch. See also **snap**.
bags of: much, a lot, a bunch, many. Curly Watts once described a young and fetching maiden as having 'bags of class'.
bang in: see **bung in**.
bang on: exactly correct. 'You're bang on there, squire.' 'I agree with you all the way.' Compare **spot on**.
bang to rights: red-handed, in an indefensible position. To *catch someone bang to rights* is to catch him in the act. Percy Sugden, on neighbourhood-watch patrol, was caught apparently bang to rights as a peeping Tom, though Percy claimed his motive was somewhat different. Nineteenth-century cant, from the idea of absolute certainty, being 'bang-on' right.
banger: an old, decrepit car. There have been several notable bangers on the Street, the most controversial being Ken Barlow's VW. Albert Tatlock refused to ride in it – not by virtue of its unroadworthy condition, but because he considered it a 'Jerry car', Annie Walker's more stately Rover, which she thought eminently suitable for Weatherfield's First Lady, rapidly became a banger under the rough handling of barman Fred Gee. A banger is also, of course, a sausage.
banjax: break, ruin, or, in the personal sense, exhaust, **knacker**. Eddie Yeats was frequently banjaxed after a day emptying dust-bins. Jack Duckworth would be banjaxed thinking about it.
bap: a barmcake of Scottish extraction; Scottish bakers are sometimes called 'bappers'.
barmcake: a soft, white-bread bun sold fresh or buttered with a choice of filling. Alf Roberts' corner shop has to date sold 21,303 barmcakes to the girls of Baldwin's Casuals. The shop offers four standard fillings – ham, cheese, meat-paste and sandwich spread. See **barmy**.
barmpot: a fool or, affectionately, one given to erratic behaviour. An airhead (see next entry).

Ena shows she has **bags of** vigour.

barmy: daft, light-headed (full of air, barm being yeast).
barney: a loud altercation one step nearer to physical violence than an **argy-bargy**. **Arguing the toss** can develop into an **argy-bargy** and then rapidly escalate into a full-blown barney. Roughly on the same decibel scale is a 'right old **ding dong**'.
Barney's goose: a person who appears to have no opinions of his own, and always agrees with whatever one says.
be: by, as in 'be now'. Overheard in the Kabin: 'Pigeon News hasn't come today luv, but it'll be here *be* tomorrow.'
be doing with: tolerating, putting up with. Percy Sugden, never one to respond eagerly to the charms of Phyllis Pearce, fended off her amorous advances with, 'Give over, woman! I can't be doing with all that nonsense.'
be for the high jump: to be obliged to face authority in a difficult or unpleasant situation. Bet Lynch told Mavis Riley 'I reckon I'm for the high jump' when she was summoned to the brewery to explain why she had deserted the Rovers (to go away, as it turned out, with a barman she had met in Blackpool).
be lucky: *You'll be lucky* – an expression of strong doubt: 'That's what you think!' For instance, 'You've fallen in love with me, right, Susan?' 'You'll be lucky!'
beans on toast: the staple diet of the Ogdens and perhaps the most popular tea-time meal in *Coronation Street*, easy to prepare and easy on the budget. Hilda often tells her lodger, Kevin: 'I won't be in for tea, chuck, but there's a tin of beans in the larder.'
beggar this for a game of soldiers: signifies that an activity has become futile or exhausting. 'To hell with this', or 'Who needs this?' *Beggar* is a euphemism for bugger, but the intimidating presence of Ena, the Street's moral watchdog, always deterred its full use. Len Fairclough and Stan Ogden commonly used the expression, which has seldom been heard since.
bell: *give someone a bell* – call someone on the telephone.
belly timber: food. An expression dating from 1600.
belter: defined by Phythian as 'an excellent thing or person'. A good joke can be a belter, as can a pretty girl or a fast greyhound.
belt up!: 'Shut up!' 'If you don't belt up I'll sew a button on it!'

berk: a stupid or disreputable person; sometimes redundantly employed as *stupid berk*. Partridge gives an obscene rhyming-slang origin ('Berkshire hunt'), but it could simply be rhyming slang or cant for 'jerk'.
best: *best bitter* – bitter beer, generic in the sense that many breweries have a 'best bitter'. This is not neccessarily superior to any other brews of bitter, it merely has a different flavour.
bevvy: general term for (alcoholic) drink. 'Are you coming for a bevvy?'
bin man: the fellow North Americans know as the garbage man. Eddie Yeats and Curly Watts were the Street's best-known bin men, based at Weatherfield Urban District Council yard. The real rubbish from *Coronation Street* is dumped at Adswood Tip, near Stockport, used as a location for bin men stories. The contents of people's dustbins are said, by psychologists, to be very revealing – a view reinforced in 1980 when Eddie disclosed the contents of Annie Walker's dustbin to Rovers regulars. Annie, furious that the *hoi polloi* should discover that she was a secret sherry-sipper, complained bitterly to the council and demanded that her bin men should be replaced. In protest, they refused to empty her bins and Annie had to pay Stan Ogden £3 to do the job for her (see **blackleg**). As argument raged, Annie discreetly slipped away to stay with her daughter Joan in Derby until the **barney** subsided.
birding: dating or picking up women. From 'bird', slang for girl.
bit of fluff, bit of stuff: comely or loose woman.
bits and bobs: odds and ends. In an especially poignant episode, Stan Ogden's bits and bobs, his spectacles, comb and other personal effects, were returned to Hilda by the hospital after his death.
black: to make persona non grata, 'blackball'.
blackguard: to be a scoundrel, or to run someone down as one. From 'the Black Guard', or soldiers of evil. Another theory is that *blackguard* originally described household servants, the guardians of the scullery, who were often covered in soot. They were prime suspects in cases of theft and other downstairs naughtiness.
blackleg: a scab, one who works while others are on strike. 1978 brought the Street's most dramatic blackleg incident when Mike Baldwin sacked cleaner Hilda Ogden because she demanded a new brush. Baldwin accused her of wilfully damaging the brush, and the girls walked out in protest, prompting Baldwin to import blackleg labour. Hilda, meanwhile, had taken a job cleaning the abbatoir offices. In 1984, Hilda's lodger Henry Wakefield was exposed as a blackleg – he had defied a strike call at Foster's Foundry. Shop steward Ivy Tilsley and the girls retaliated by forcing him out of a job at Baldwin's. See **send someone to Coventry.**
black pudding: dish made from pig's blood, oats and fat. Found mainly in the north of England and Brittany.
blatherskite: someone who talks incessantly. From 'blather' – to say much of little worth. From the U.S.
bleeding heck: a euphemistic version of bloody hell and one of the strongest ways to show you are in a mood to invoke the devil without actually taking the plunge. ('Flippin' 'eck' is less bold, and 'oh 'eck' is downright wishy-washy.) The restrained language of *Coronation Street* stems less from any sense of propriety than an attempt at depicting an ingrained reluctance to swear among older working class people. Younger characters in the series speak more freely, and are therefore perhaps less imaginative when using oaths. The Street's more familiar faces tend to stick to *'eck* for 'hell', as in *flippin' 'eck*, or 'Will I *'eck* as like!' *Bleedin' 'eck* did pass the lips of Eddie Yeats, however, on a few occasions. In a terraced street a veneer of respectability always prevails over violent emotion, part of the deep-rooted code

Blacklegs at Baldwin's Casuals.

which decrees that you can have milk bottles on the table so long as you cannot see them through the lace curtains. See **bloody** for a more detailed history of swearing in *Coronation Street*.

blimey o'reilly: occasionally used by Hilda Ogden and Elsie Tanner. *Blimey* is of course a venerable oath, a contraction of 'Blind me!' – as in 'Gor blimey!' – 'God strike me blind if it isn't true.' This non-blasphemous version may have come from Ireland, although blasphemy expert Reinhold Aman (yes, there are such people) cites Hungary as the most blasphemous country in the world.

blinder: someone impressive, derived from the idea of dazzling, really shining. To *play a blinder*, a phrase of sporting origin, means to perform outstandingly. Compare **belter**, **bobby dazzler**.

blinkin': like **bleeding**, a euphemistic form of the intensive **bloody**.

bloody: *bloody hell* – the strongest of *Coronation Street* oaths and, in the early days, one of the rarest. The expression was used only once in the first twelve years of the series, on October 1, 1962, when Harry Hewitt vowed what he would do to the person who had kidnapped his baby son Christopher – 'I'll wring his bloody neck!' Expletives such as 'ecky thump', 'flippin' 'eck', 'blinkin' 'eck', 'bloomin' 'eck' and 'oh 'eck' were frequently used during the years of abstinence. Then, in 1972, there was almost a profusion of bloodys. In January, Alan Howard had a row with Billy Walker, who had sold the garage they jointly owned without consulting him, and told him he had 'no bloody right'. A month later Ernest Bishop, perhaps the least profane of Street residents, was furious that the arrival of Emily's infirm Auntie May had caused their wedding to be postponed. 'I'm bloody fed up', he told a rather shocked Emily. Bloody was again used in September by a policeman investigating the kidnap of

Ena's grandson, Jason Lomax, who vanished while she was at Preston Guild. But it was two years before bloody surfaced again, when garage customer Stewart Draper angrily sought out Billy Walker who had sold him a white Alfa for £1,300. The car was an insurance write-off worth less than £500. Unbridled emotion or a deep sense of injustice were considered the only suitable setting for its use. In August 1974, Ray Langton pushed back the boundaries further when he mused with Jerry Booth, over a cup of tea in the cafe, that when he was dead people would remember him as 'a right bloody old git'. ('Bloody' and 'git' used in conjunction were the strongest language heard in fourteen years of *Coronation Street*.) The occasion was eclipsed only in 1975, when Len Fairclough found the body of a dead woman at the foot of his stairs. Her husband, Ray Johnson, was arrested and led away by police shouting 'You bastards!' Since then, depending on the discretion of the producer, 'bloody' or 'bloody hell' has been used more frequently to keep abreast of changing times. The *Oxford English Dictionary* defines the phrase with profound repugnance and tells us – quite unreasonably, really – that there is no reason to believe that the oath has blasphemous roots in 'Sblood – 'God's blood!' or 'Christ's blood!' – familiar from Shakespeare. Another not unreasonable etymology is that *bloody* is a contraction of 'By Our Lady', but the O.E.D. prefers links with 'young bloods', seventeenth-century ruffians. 'The phrase "bloody drunk" was apparently equivalent to "as drunk as a blood". . . thence it was extended to kindred expressions, and at length to others.' It is said that many of those who attended the original staging of Shaw's *Pygmalion* paid their admission just for the pleasure of gasping in shock when Eliza Dolittle used the word. See **bleeding heck, ha-bloody-ha**.

blot one's copybook: lose someone's affection or favour, or make a serious error. George Wardle 'blotted his copybook' with Ivy Tilsley when it was revealed that he had been divorced, and therefore he and Ivy could not have a wedding in the Catholic Church.

blow: a mild expletive, usually followed by a noun, along the lines of 'to heck with'. 'Isn't Emily coming?' 'Oh, blow Emily!' Also, *to be blowed* – 'I'm blowed if I'm eating humble pie for Mike Baldwin!'

blubber: cry. Some of the ladies of *Coronation Street* are prone to a discreet blubber when watching weddings. Common expression in North America.

bobby dazzler: a source of great pride, often directed at children: 'Young Nicky's a real bobby dazzler'.

bog: an outdoor toilet, privy. Despite modernization, all the houses in *Coronation Street* still retain a backyard outhouse. (See **cludgy** – the doors, by the way, are generally a muddy brown, with the exception of the Ogdens' who, in an unceasing quest for style, painted theirs purple.) Ken Barlow was the first to have an indoor lavatory installed, to comply with health regulations when his wife Valerie opened a hairdressing business at home. When, many years later, Alf Roberts' wife Audrey followed suit and washed her clients' hair in the bathroom sink, Alf found access to his own lavatory barred at a time of urgent need. A *bog* may also be referred to as a *carsey,* sometimes spelt kharzi, a term of obscure origin. Formerly, all were equipped with *bog paper* ('Bronco' was a popular semi-glazed brand), either nailed to the door in single sheets, or on a roll which was kept indoors to avoid mildew and was carried down the yard for each separate visit. *Bog off*, meaning 'get lost', was a phrase occasionally used by Stan Ogden, and also Eddie Yeats, who uttered more oaths than any other Street character. The old verb *to bog*, to relieve one's bowels, has yet to be heard in *Coronation Street*.

boil: to dispute, get into an **argy bargy**. As in 'my blood boiled'. See **potboiler**.

bomb: describes wealth or success: see **go down a bomb**, **make a bomb**.

bounden duty: solemn duty. A serious phrase with religious overtones first used by Ena Sharples and, nowadays, by Hilda Ogden when moralizing.
box clever: play it cool, craftily, play one's options carefully. Jack Duckworth's entire married life with Vera is a text book example of boxing clever. He is, however, occasionally too clever for his own good. See **clever clogs**.
brainbox: the locus of intelligence, indicating that one has more than empty space between the ears. As in 'He's a real brainbox – he always did well at Bessie Street.' Also, an especially intelligent person. Ken Barlow and Curly Watts are the Street's most prolific brainboxes, although, generally the Street does not fare well in cerebral matters. The Rovers has lost every quiz competition against the Flying Horse and the Swan – a source of immense satisfaction to landladies Nellie Harvey and Stella Rigby. The closest call was during the 1985 Brainiest Pub Competition, when Rita, Mavis, Percy and Ken were fielded against some formidable intellects recruited by Stella Rigby of the Swan. The Rovers lost 46-45 after serious disagreement over who scored the hat-trick for England in the 1966 World Cup.
brainstorm: having a brainstorm on *Coronation Street* is a less positive experience than in those parts of the world where it denotes innovation or inspiration (see **brainwave**). On the Street, the word is taken literally, to mean an explosion of anger, or to become loudly irate.
brainwave: a clever idea. Dennis Tanner was over-endowed with brainwaves, which included taking a chimp as a lodger, keeping a performing seal in the bath for commercial gain, and managing a stripper, Eunice 'La Composita' Bond, and her pet python.
brass: for possibly 600 years or more, an expression synonymous with money. Originally from brass or copper coins.
bread and scrape: bread and dripping. See **butty**.

'You might have expected **bread and scrape**, luv, but I think *coq-au-vin*'s more romantic.'

breakdown van: tow truck. Residents still refer to Brian Tilsley's truck as a van, even though the garage has not operated one for many years. Brian bought the current model second hand for £1,500 in 1985 and immediately ran into trouble when he parked it outside his council house in Hamilton Road. Neighbour Ernie Ratcliffe, who had just bought his home from the council, insisted that Brian should move the truck six feet as it was lowering the tone of his property.
brew up: make tea. Len Fairclough's yard was once a focal point of the ancient Weatherfield brewing up ceremony. These days Phyllis and Gail are said to dispense the best brew, at Jim's Cafe.

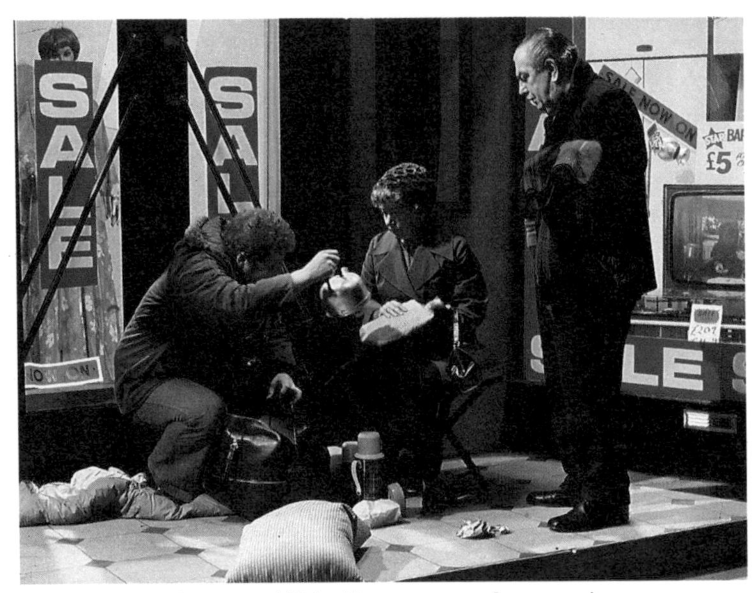

'Come on, Hilda. It's your turn to **brew up**.'

broad: *to talk broad* – To talk in a northern way, with broadly-sounded (open) vowels. To southerners and uppity northerners, talking broad is uncouth.
broody: the state of brooding, or seeming to, as in, 'What's up wi' you? You look broody.' The expression should be used with caution as it can also apply to a woman whose maternal stirrings create a yearning to have a baby.
brush: *to live over the brush* – to live as man and wife while unmarried. (See **over the brush**.)
buckle to: buckle down, become serious about, as in, 'If we buckle to we'll have this job finished by dinner.'
buffer: an eccentric or foolish old man. 'Silly old buffer' is occasionally used on the Street to describe officious community centre caretaker Percy Sugden.
bung: give or pass. When Jack Duckworth became cellarman at the Rovers he asked Bet Lynch to 'bung a few extra quid' into his pay packet. *Bung in* means to make a formal claim or application – for example, to bung in a claim for Social Security or insurance.
bunk: slang of over 100 years vintage meaning to leave hastily, often, to *do a bunk*, as in the manner of Dennis Tanner. Partridge says it comes from America. Compare **do a flit** and **sling one's hook**. To **skive-off** is generally applied to one who is absent from work.
Burtonwood: U.S.A.F. base near Warrington which provided a transit camp for

thousands of G.I.s during World War II. Master Sgt. Steve Tanner, one of Elsie's former husbands, was stationed there.
buskin' it: improvising. From busking, performing or selling something in the streets on the move; for example, someone unexpectedly stopped by the police while carrying stolen goods may 'busk it' when questioned. Busking was once used to describe the cruising of ships, especially pirate ships.
bust-up: a really nasty argument, sometimes ending in violence. A 'knock-down-drag-out' quarrel as North Americans vividly term it; the final stage in the escalation which begins with **arguing the toss**. The pavements of *Coronation Street* have witnessed several bust-ups over the years.
buttered doorsteps: thick sandwiches of the type made by hungry children on arrival from school. Sandwich thickness on the Street can be aligned with intellectual capacity – 'He's as thick as Jim's butties', Jim's being the local cafe.
butty: a sandwich, generally on buttered bread. Stan Ogden, whose eating habits were very basic, had a great enthusiasm for 'chip butties' – white sliced bread crammed with French-fried potatoes. Boiled ham sandwiches cut diagonally are standard fare at *Coronation Street* funerals, or with the crust cut off if the mourners are well-to-do. Sherry and meat-paste sandwiches are usually provided as a 'running buffet' to celebrate wedding anniversaries.
Annie Walker was considered the greatest living authority on the art of sandwich-making. She would have considered jam butties vulgar (see **common**), and sugar or sauce butties beneath contempt. *Sarnies* are the Liverpudlian equivalent of butties.
by a long chalk: by a great deal. From the use of chalk in keeping score during games. Are Jack and Vera a lovely couple? 'Not by a long chalk.'
by the cringe: an oath, of obscure origin.
by the heck, by the left: euphemisms for 'hell'. Compare **Gordon Bennett!**
by your leave: without apology or explanation. 'Don't talk to me about vets! Without so much as a by-your-leave he threw our budgie on the fire and said "That'll be eight and sixpence for cremation."'

A Street **bust-up**.

cack-handed: clumsy. 'Cowboy' workmen occasionally descend on the Street and do 'cack-handed', or shoddy, house repairs. An earlier meaning was 'left-handed' (compare with 'left-footer' for Roman Catholic), the earlier form 'gawk-handed'. 'Gawk' is still used for idiot, or fool, in Weatherfield. See **gawp**.
caf: cafe. The best-known on *Coronation Street* is Jim's, on Rosamund Street, across the road from Rita Fairclough's Kabin. Jim's is sometimes referred to by older residents as Dawson's. Egg and chips, mugs of tea and sausage butties are the most profitable lines.
calf-lick: tuft of rebellious hair which refuses to lie down at the front of the head. The American equivalent is cow-lick. See also **cat lick**.
call someone, call something: To tell someone what's what about their behaviour; denigrate, criticize. 'Calling someone' behind their back is an unacceptable character trait. Hilda, for instance, never 'called Stan' in front of others, while Jack and Vera Duckworth 'call' each other all the time.
camp: to overstay one's welcome, or fail to take the hint to leave. 'Ivy came and camped on us all Sunday afternoon.' Also, to chat idly over a cup of tea. Lancashire textile mills used to have large notices warning: 'No Camping'.
caned: to be admonished, to take abuse. 'He could hardly stand up when he left the Rovers. I bet he got a right caning when he got home.' To take a caning in speculative business dealings has the same sense as getting one's fingers burned, or, in North America, 'taking a beating'.
caper: vague reference to any subject or ongoing concern. Comparable to what North Americans call 'business'. Jack Duckworth reflects on a possible career as a publican: 'This pub caper's a doddle, Vera.'
carry-on: a fuss, a 'lot of bother'. 'There'll be a right carry-on when Mike Baldwin knows you borrowed the firm's van, George.'
carry the can: to take the blame for. Possibly from the custom of miners carrying explosives to the coal face in a tin can. Hence everyone is reluctant to 'carry the can'.
carsey: see **bog.**
cat lick: a lock of a boy's or man's hair plastered down on forehead.
cha: tea. From both the Hindu and Mandarin Chinese, and, according to the O.E.D., used in English to describe a cuppa since 1616. Cup for cup, Hilda, Percy and Phyllis are the Street's biggest tea consumers.
chairs – to have all one's chairs at home: to be alert, on guard, of quick intelligence, mindful; to 'play with a full deck'. 'Our Sharon's doing well for herself, she's courting a computer programmer.' 'My, she's got her chairs at home.'
chalk and cheese: *as like (or as different) as chalk and cheese* – 'Chalk and cheese are opposed in various proverbial expressions as things differing greatly in qualities or value,' – when in appearance they seem quite similar (O.E.D.).

champion: fine, grand, well. 'Hey up, Albert! You look champion today.'
chance'd be a fine thing: spoken with irony, as with the North American 'Sure thing'. 'If I come up on the coupon this weekend I'll buy myself a pub.' 'Chance'd be a fine thing.' The emphasis is on improbability, not likelihood.
(a) change is as good as a rest: popular saying in Weatherfield, where holidays can be few and far between.
chara: a holiday or excursion bus. From the French *char à banc* (pronounced 'charabang' in Weatherfield). A coach with benches, popular in the 1920s. Essential travel accessories on a chara (pronounced 'sharra' or 'chaira') are a thermos of tea and chopped egg butties. Courting couples, or large gentlemen carrying crates of brown ale, traditionally favour the back seat. Ena once returned with a face like thunder after being left behind on a chara trip to Blackpool illuminations.
cheek: common Britishism for impudence or smart-alecky behaviour, as in, 'Don't give me any of your cheek!' or 'Do you believe the cheek of her!' Possibly derived from turning one's face brazenly full-beam on someone while being insolent. Partridge compares it to *lip*, as in *give someone lip*. Hilda frequently accuses lippy people – or indeed anyone who disagrees with her – of having 'the cheek of the Devil'.
cheeky monkey: smart aleck, someone who makes brash remarks or gets up to brash tricks. Often said, with more affection than censure, of precocious children. A favourite phrase of Betty Turpin.
chin-wag: a conversation, a chat. 'Chinwaggin'' in the sense of gossiping is sometimes called 'gabbin''.
chippate: cock-up, mess, from slang used by soldiers stationed in India. In their ignorance, the soldiers thought that Indian cookery, which involved throwing many ingredients into a pan, was devoid of any art.
chippin' it: eating food from a *chippy* (fish and chip shop), or other fast-food establishment. Chips are the most popular item of food in Weatherfield. The finest come from Jackson's chippy in Rosamund Street, although Hilda's brother, Archie Crabtree, was said to 'do a nice fish' at his chippy just outside Weatherfield. Frank Jackson offers a 'special' or fish cake, and a 'split' – fish, chips and mushy peas, in addition to bottles of Vimto, a fruity-tasting mineral water.
chippy: see previous entry.
chuck: venerable term of affection or endearment, used most famously by Lady Macbeth. Stan was Hilda's 'chuck', and 'Hiya, chuck!' is Vera Duckworth's favourite form of greeting.
chuck someone: jilt someone. See **kick someone into touch**.
chuck up: give up, cast aside: 'He's chucked up his girlfriend.' Rita, for instance, was on the verge of a promising career as a nightclub singer but could never bring herself to 'chuck up the day job'. From 'chuck in the sponge', a boxing term (akin to 'throw in the towel') meaning to withdraw from the contest. See **jack it in**.
chucky egg (pronounced 'chooky')**:** a hen's egg. Chucky is a northern children's expression for chicken or other fowl, thought to be taken from the clucking sound they make. 'Chuck' in this sense is recorded from the seventeenth century.
chuffed: delighted, happy. Being extremely chuffed is sometimes described as being 'chuffed as 'owt'. The expression, which dates from the 1860s, can also be used in mild sarcasm, as when Bet Lynch, an expert at all forms of sarcasm, is 'chuffed to little mint balls'.
chunner: to mutter, complain. Often directed at someone who constantly moans at the state of the world – 'What are you chunnerin' about now, Albert?' Also *chunter*.
clack: to talk or chatter incessantly. *To take clack*, therefore, is to take verbal flak.

'Course I'll come, Stella. I'm **chuffed to little mint-balls**.'

clap eyes on: to see, 'especially unexpectedly or finally' (Partridge). 'I haven't clapped eyes on Leonard Swindley for **yonks**.'
clapped-out: worn out, obsolete.
clarty: dirty, soiled. 'Slutchy', meaning muddy, may also be used. Of obscure origin.
clat-tale: A tell-tale ('tattle-tale' in North America); children's expression.
clemmed: hungry, 'starved through', as Hilda Ogden says. 'What's in the larder, chuck? I'm clemmed.'
clever clogs: a witty person, or more commonly, one who thinks he is; a smart-aleck or 'smarty pants', someone who is 'so sharp he'll cut himself'. Not an indication of intelligence; thus Ken Barlow is not a clever clogs, but Terry Duckworth frequently is.
clever dick: similar to **clever clogs**, although perhaps less jocular.
clock: see, observe; e.g., 'Did you clock that judy (girl)?'
clock on: to punch a card in a time-clock on arriving and leaving work. Baldwin's Casuals insist that the girls clock-on and off. The North American equivalent is 'punch in'.
club: see **in the club.**
club man: door-to-door insurance collector who calls weekly for premium installments. In Weatherfield and surrounding areas, penny-a-week policies to take care of one's own funeral arrangements are considered a praiseworthy precaution.
cludgy: an outdoor toilet. Stan Ogden retained a great affection for his cludgy, preferring to use it long after Hilda had an indoor version installed. A query by the author to E. C. Dann, assistant editor of the *New Oxford Dictionary*, has turned up no such usages of cludgy outside *Coronation Street.* Possessing a clean cludgy was a source of pride to Hilda Ogden who, in common with other Street residents,

touched up any flaking whitewash and always ensured that there were fresh squares of the *Gazette* on the nail. 'Cludgy', Dann writes, 'has been found as an adjective meaning "thick, sticky" or as an adverb, "heavily, stickily".'
cob on: *to have a cob on* – to be irritable or crusty.
cobblers: see **codswallop**.
cock: widely used on *Coronation Street*, especially by Bet Lynch, to mean mate, pal or buddy, as in, 'Hiya, cock!' Akin to **chuck**, and directed at men and women alike.
cock of the dunghill: ironic form, of course, of *cock of the walk*. Equivalent to the North American 'big cheese', 'top banana', or someone who thinks he is.
cock's stride: a very short distance. Ken and Deirdre Barlow live 'nobbut a cock's stride' from the Rovers – just next door.
codology: hokum, bumf or intentional deception. Compare next entry.
codswallop: Nonsense, as in 'a load of old codswallop'. Along with 'a load of old cobblers', the expression may have obscene origins having to do with male genitalia. Another suggested etymology is Codd's ginger beer (Codd invented the

'One day I'll have me own little place, with an indoor **cludgy**.'

pressurized beverage bottle) and wallop, an old term for beer – 'fool's beer', or something patently full of froth or fizz and not to be taken seriously.
collywobbles: stomach ache or, more generally, 'a disordered state of the stomach characterized by rumbling in the intestines'. The expression also means a state of being nervous and 'having butterflies', a condition with which Mavis Riley has been afflicted most of her life. An article in *Punch*, for October 9 1841, tells of someone trying not to get 'the collywobbles in his pandenoodles' – pandenoodles being a nonsense word for intestines.
come the: affect, as in **come the acid**; to treat someone scathingly or sarcastically. Another meaning implies fake or pretence – someone 'coming the innocent' to avoid blame or, in the case of Jack Duckworth, 'coming the invalid' to avoid work.

Emily has a bad case of the **collywobbles**.

come a cropper: take a heavy fall, have a bad accident. Perhaps from horse-riding or hunting – to fall with the crop in your hand? Jack Duckworth came a nasty cropper off his window-cleaning ladder in Dulcie Frogitt's front garden.
come it: to try to put one over, to cheat someone. From the early 1880s and perpetuated by Len Fairclough – 'Don't come it with me, pal!' Mike Baldwin 'comes it a bit strong' with the girls when important orders have to be completed on time, but he 'isn't as bad as he's painted'.
come through: the *Coronation Street* version of 'come in'. An expression to be taken literally – the everyday room was traditionally the kitchen, accessible only by walking from the front door through the living room.
come to that: 'when all is said and done', 'to be absolutely candid'. Milkman's daughter Andrea Clayton told her boyfriend, Terry Duckworth, 'I'm sick and tired of exams. I'm sick and tired of school, come to that.'
common: low life, a person considered to have appalling taste and dubious lifestyle. The social rule in Weatherfield is to pretend to be on a social rung higher than you in fact are, and never admit that your circumstances may have caused you to slip lower. 'Common' is a derisive term aimed at all with 'airs and graces' beyond their station, or those who dress up with more pretension to style than they may actually possess. As in, 'all fur coat and no knickers', or 'mutton dressed as lamb' (see **dolled up**). Thus, Annie Walker considered Elsie Tanner to be 'rather common' and Elsie, in turn, thought Hilda Ogden to be 'a bit common'. Hilda saw Elsie as 'proper common', but not Annie Walker. Vera Duckworth, on the other hand, is considered 'common' by everyone. Paradoxically, Bet Lynch's leopardskin coat might be 'common' in Weatherfield, but trendy in London. This means – a confusing point for outsiders, here – that Bet's coat is literally uncommon in Coronation Street, but common among New Wave enthusiasts in London. If

something, therefore, is 'common' it is quite likely to be uncommon – unlike Vera who is reassuringly 'common' all the time. For those interested in the fine-tuning of such matters, Jack Duckworth, who likes wearing medallions and slashed-to-the-waist shirts, is 'dead common', while Vera, by common consent, is 'as common as muck'. Being 'common' is clearly in the eye of the beholder. *Common* is also widely used in North America.

conk: nose, sometimes head. Partridge suggests it comes from 'conch', a shell. Albert Tatlock's distinctive conk was probably acquired through his dedication to rum.

cop: catch out, discover, capture, grab. A *fair cop*: someone who is justly caught out, or arrested. For the statistically-inclined, 63 cops have appeared in *Coronation Street*, along with 17 clergymen, 36 ambulancemen and 10 fire-engines.

cop for it: to succeed or win; also sometimes simply to take, possibly from racecourse slang.

copperplate: precise penmanship, of the type once taught at Bessie Street School.

cork-legged: see **keg-legged.**

cost a packet: see **make a packet**.

council flat; council house: housing provided at low cost to the working class, subsidized by the local authority. Of the *Coronation Street* characters, only Brian and Gail Tilsley now live in a council house. Ken Barlow lived in a council maisonette when he first married, and sold his Mini to furnish it. Percy Sugden, as a council employee looking after the community centre, lives in council accommodation.

coventry: see **send someone to Coventry**.

crack it: succeed after effort. 'A new car? No problem, mate. Come up with five thousand quid and you've cracked it.' Also, succeed amorously. Perhaps from the idea of cracking through a door or barrier.

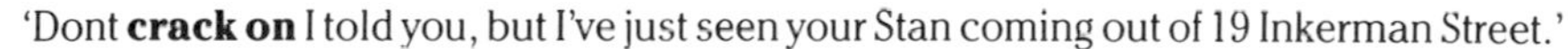

'Dont **crack on** I told you, but I've just seen your Stan coming out of 19 Inkerman Street.'

crack on: pretend, but also, paradoxically, 'divulge'. 'Crack on I didn't tell you' has the same meaning, oddly enough, as the negative 'don't crack on about it'. Both convey 'don't let it be known that. . .'. Possibly from *crack*, to boast, itself from *crack* meaning 'to make a sharp noise'.
cracking: lively, excellent, grand; as in, 'a really cracking time'.
cracking the flags: very sunny: 'It's cracking the flags out there.'
create: kick up (create) a fuss. 'He was creating in the Rovers, so Bet barred him out.'
credit it: believe, find credible. 'Would you credit it, eh?' is an expression of incredulity or exasperation.
cry off: back out, withdraw at the last moment, make an excuse. Derek, for instance, 'cried off' from marrying Mavis.
cuppa: a cup of tea. Street residents have great faith in the restorative properties of a cuppa. After a heavy shopping expedition ladies have been seen to collapse into chairs gasping: 'Ooh, my corns are throbbing. I could murder a cuppa'. As a panacea, nothing has quite surpassed the effects of 'a good lie down and a nice cuppa tea'.
cut: canal or – off the Street – other channel of water, from the idea that it was cut out of the earth. The local canal has been the focal point for many *Coronation Street* dramas when someone wants to be alone and think things out.
cut ice with: impress, make a difference to. 'All his education cuts no ice with me – it's *experience* what counts.' Originated in America, but is no longer common there.

dab hand: someone skilled or clever at something. Curly Watts, for instance, is said to be a 'dab hand' at astronomy – a dubious accolade – just as Len Fairclough was a 'dab hand' at carpentry. Jack Duckworth, on the other hand, has never been a 'dab hand' at anything, especially electrics.
daily: the daily cleaning woman. Hilda Ogden has been cleaning since 1964 when Martha Longhurst died in the Snug, and Hilda took over her job at the Rovers. Ten years later, Hilda joined the Seamen's Union and attempted to polish her way round the world as a cleaner on the cruise liner M.V. Monteumbe. It was on this epic voyage that she acquired a taste for Planter's Punch and entertaining on a grand scale (see **afters**). Since then, with the aplomb only a juggler could muster, she has managed to keep a record number of cleaning jobs going at one time. At full capacity Hilda has scurried with her dusters from Benny Lewis's betting shop, to the Rovers, to Mike Baldwin's flat, to the clothing factory – all the while working simultaneously as a cloak-room attendant at Baldwin's Graffitti Club. Her calf muscles, though never displayed in public, are reputed to be like whip-cords.
dead: really, very. An intensive adjective now deadeningly common in Britain, and often sounding quite incongruous if taken literally. In, 'he's dead handsome', for example, the person spoken of would, generally-speaking, be far from inanimate. Again, as man-hungry widow Phyllis Pearce said after a pleasant evening with retired property-owner Sam Tindall, 'It were dead romantic'; and pop singer Brett Falcon – also known as local window cleaner Walter Potts – was regarded as 'dead sexy' by Lucille Hewitt in 1963.
deadleg: an ineffectual, useless, or unmotivated person; a dead beat.
decko (also dekko): visual observation, as in, 'have a decko' – have a look. From Hindu/Romany, via Gypsies.
dicky, dicky bird: rhyming slang for 'word'. 'Any news from Elsie since she went to Portugal?' 'Not a dicky bird.' *Dicky* also means unhealthy or below par in reference to a specific part of the body. Curly Watts, before he resigned from the bins, stayed off work with a 'dicky back', a condition which also afflicted Stan Ogden and has been known to keep Jack Duckworth from exerting himself. There was once concern that Len Fairclough had a 'dicky ticker', or heart malfunction, but he was found to be suffering from simple overwork. Possibly the most medically-baffling and longest-running affliction suffered by any Street character was Albert Tatlock's 'moving shrapnel'. After years of physical discomfort it was discovered to be a piece of German shell which had lodged in his backside during trench warfare in 1916. The offending foreign body was successfully removed by surgery at Weatherfield Hospital. On his return Albert found little comfort in rumours circulating the Rovers that, in view of the evidence, he could only have been wounded running from the guns. Annie Walker, strictly speaking, did not have any 'dicky' parts, but a history of

Albert Tatlock — a martyr to 'moving shrapnel'.

recurring migraine. She would often retire from the bar with 'one of her heads'.
digs: lodgings, flat, apartment. From 'diggings'. Curly Watts is 'in digs' with widow Emily Bishop.
dimp: cigarette butt.
ding-dong: violent shouting-match, altercation. 'There's a right old ding-dong going on outside No.9.'
dishy: comely, attractive, looking delicious. Terry Duckworth, for instance, is convinced that the entire female population of Weatherfield finds him 'dishy'.
dish up: meals are rarely served in *Coronation Street*, but always 'dished up'. Commonly used in U.S. and Canada.
do: a social gathering, party or other celebratory get-together. Catering at any of Annie Walker's 'do's' was always of the highest standard. To emphasize that quality, rather than quantity, was essential to any proper do, Annie specialized in *vol-au-vents*. The most frantic preparation for a do may often be disguised by the modesty of the invitation, as was the case of Stella Rigby at the Swan: 'I'm having a little do for

Elsie has a bit of a **do**.

the Lady Victuallers tonight, Bet dear. Try to drop by if you can. . .' Other usages describe a state of affairs – 'that were a poor do' – or waft a hint of scandal, as in, 'that were a bit of a rum do'.
do a bomb: do extremely (explosively) well. Alf Roberts' shop has been doing a bomb since it was modernized. Compare **go down a bomb** and **make a bomb.**
do a flit: 'do a bunk', run off, disappear overnight. Also known in *Coronation Street* as 'moon flettin'.
do (someone) down: criticize, double deal, cheat. See **call**.
do for: to clean for someone, or act as caretaker or landlady. When Stan died, Hilda took in a lodger because she missed having someone to do for.
do foreigners: to use the boss's time and materials for one's own gain. Partridge gives its origin as military slang for 'an article made in the Service's time and with its own materials'. But the expression may have roots in the idea of cheap foreign labour. Garageman Brian Tilsley has accused his mechanic Kevin of doing foreigners on friends' cars.
do one's whack: do one's share. See **whack.**
do someone (oneself) proud: behave in a way that reflects well on oneself or

others. The list of people Hilda Ogden admires makes a slim volume but, on encountering them she says: 'You do yourself proud'.
do the dirty on someone: do something unkind to someone, **do someone down**.
do up a treat: dress or prepare attractively. See **treat**.
dobby horse: an old expression for fairground roundabout, or ride. Used by Albert Tatlock, Hilda Ogden and Ena Sharples.

'You **did us proud**, Hilda luv. I just need a bit of a lie down after them eggs in aspic.'

doddle: something easy, requiring little physical or mental effort.
dodgy: dangerous, questionable, 'iffy'. Vera Duckworth found that having a television without a licence was 'pretty dodgy' when she was fined £150. The Duckworths, who had expected to be fined £250, celebrated their relief with drinks. Jack had one too many and fell over the TV set, damaging it beyond repair.
doesn't one just: ironic agreement with what has been said. As in, 'I know you hate to leave the ironing for a night out.' 'Oh, don't I just!'
dog's body: someone detailed to do all the trivial, menial, but nonetheless crucial, tasks in an enterprise. Also a well-meaning person whose willingness is imposed upon. Sometimes referred to as a 'skivvy', and, in North America, a 'gofer' (one who 'goes for' this and that).
dog's dinner: *done up like a dog's dinner* – 'Dressed to kill', dressed stylishly.
dog warden: dog catcher. When Phyllis threatened to bash Percy Sugden with a dish in Jim's cafe, he warned her he would call the dog warden.
dolled up: dressed in one's best clothes, or finery, for a special occasion. As in,

'Where's she off to, all dolled up?' The word formally became British in 1934 when published in an appendix of mostly U.S. expressions in the *Concise Oxford Dictionary.*

Bet, all **dolled up.**

dollop: a shapeless lump. As in, 'Sausage, egg and a dollop of mashed potato, Phyllis luv.' In everyday use in North America.
dolly blue: a blue twist of fabric containing an agent for whitening clothes.
donkey stone: a soft stone used to colour or whiten a doorstep or window-sill. Popular in the early days of *Coronation Street*, and obtained from rag-and-bone carts, which were originally drawn by donkeys. In exchange for rags or scrap iron, housewives could choose between a donkey stone and a bottle of bleach. Today, these have been replaced by balloons or goldfish in plastic bags. Hilda Ogden, like many Weatherfield residents, was an enthusiastic donkey stone user, whitening not only her front doorstep, but also the paving stones and kerb in front of her house, to give it an air of cleanliness and respectability.
donkey's years: a long time. See **yonks**.
doolally: mad, crazy. From Deolali, a turn-of-the-century Bombay sanatorium where many British soldiers were detained before being shipped home. Many evidently went 'stir-crazy' with boredom.
doorstep: a thick slice of bread. A 'couple of doorsteps' is a sandwich. From about 1885. See **buttered doorstep**.
dosser: tramp, habitué of doss-houses. From mid-nineteenth century.
down to: to the credit, or blame, of someone. If the responsibility falls on no one but yourself, then 'it's all down to you'.

'I think your singing sent her **doolally** Hilda.'

drawing in: describes the decrease of daylight hours as winter approaches, as in 'the nights are drawing in'.
drinkins: a rarely used expression for a workman's dinner, once popular with Len Fairclough and Ray Langton. **Snap** has a similar meaning.
drive pigs: snore, the full expression being 'drive one's pigs to market'. Stan Ogden was often driving pigs when he slept.
drop lucky: to drop into luck, have unusual or unexpected good fortune.
drop someone: knock someone down with a punch. In North American vernacular, 'deck' someone.
drop someone in it: land someone in trouble.
dropped on: *to be dropped on* – to be surprised, often by an unexpected visit, as in, 'I could have died of shame. The house was upside down and they all dropped on us from Cleethorpes.' Also, to be at a loss for words.
duck-egg: a person of little wit or intelligence; a 'zero-brain'. From a duck, or zero score, in cricket. The North American equivalent is 'goose-egg'.

early days: indicates 'It's too soon to tell'.
earn one's corn: earn one's keep.
earwig: eavesdrop. An expression which dates from at least 1837, and an occupation at which few are more skilled than Hilda Ogden. As she earwigs while cleaning the Rovers, the more tantalizing the gossip, the faster she polishes, to appear not to be wiggling her ears into other people's business.
easy on!: Steady on! 'Take it easy!'.
Eccles cake: round, currant-filled pastry, originally from the town of Eccles, near Weatherfield. The *Coronation Street* archives reveal that in 1902, on the day the Rovers Return opened for the first time, a little boy sat on the step of the house next door, watching the ceremony as he chewed an Eccles cake. It was Albert Tatlock, who retained a great affection for them for the rest of his life. Regarded as a great Weatherfield delicacy, along with tripe, pig's trotters, black-puddings, **parkin** and **simnel cake**.
'ecky thump!: a euphemistic exclamation particularly favoured by Elsie Tanner.
eee: a tonal affirmative which can be modulated to denote affection, as in, 'Eee, our Tracy, you're making a bonny girl', or wistful chiding, as in, 'Eee, Brian, there are times when I could wring your neck'. Its subtleties are best illustrated in the story of the man who ordered a headstone for his late wife's grave with the inscription: 'She was thine'. When he came to collect it the stonemason had inscribed, 'She was thin'. The furious widower told him that he had missed the 'e' out. 'Don't worry', said the mason, 'Come back tomorrow and it'll be fixed.' When the customer returned, his wife's epitaph read: 'Eee, she was thin'.
elevenses: morning coffee or tea break, sometimes accompanied by cake or biscuits. Elevenses, or mid-morning break at Baldwin's Casuals is at 11 a.m. sharp. One minute over and there is mutiny.
'em: them. Looked upon in more educated parts of Britain (see **quality folk**) as ignorant or lazy use of the language. In defence of Coronation Street as she is spoke, it should be pointed out that this is quite erroneous. According to Dr Peter Wright, senior lecturer in modern languages at Salford University, *'em* originates from the Old English *hem*, while *them* is a much later import from Scandinavia.
E.P.N.S.: electro-plated nickel silver eating utensils – an imitation of genuine silver service.

face as long as Wigan Pier: a sad, melancholy appearance. The phrase is said with a touch of humour, because Wigan – just half an hour's drive from Weatherfield – does not have a pier. The town, which, thanks to comedian George Formby, became a music hall stereotype for small towns and provincial thinking, lies on the Leeds-Liverpool Canal. There is a small wharf for loading coal which Formby affectionately christened Wigan Pier. The sobriquet inspired the title of George Orwell's *The Road To Wigan Pier*, concerned, like *Coronation Street*, with working-class life, albeit the very brutal one of miners during the Depression.
face like a wet week: another melancholy metaphor in the vein of *face as long as a fiddle, face as long as Wigan pier.*

Elsie with a **face like a wet week**.

facer: a shock, something to wipe the smile off one's face. 'It's a bit of a facer' Jack Duckworth said solemnly to Bet Lynch when the Rovers burned down. From slang for a blow to the face.
faff: often, faff about. Fuss, dither.
fair cop: see **cop**.
fair do's: the meaning can vary according to context, from 'fair enough', indicating assent, to the adjuration 'Be fair', give one one's due.
fall off a lorry: euphemism describing something stolen or obtained by illicit means. 'Where did you get the suede jacket, Mike?' 'Let's just say it fell off the back of a lorry. . .'
fall out with: to have words with, to become angry at; as in, 'What's wrong with Gail? Has she fallen out with Brian?'
fall off his (or her) perch: die. Pet birds, especially budgerigars, being household favourites in Britain.
fancy!: 'Imagine that!' Often preceded by *'Eee'*.
fancy dan: a lover, a 'fancy man', not so much a man of showy tastes, or a 'ladies man', but one who is *fancied* by women. Jack Duckworth is Dulcie Frogget's 'fancy man'. Dulcie, in turn, is Jack's 'fancy woman', more commonly known as his 'fancy piece'.
fancy one's chances: believe that one stands a chance romantically with another person, or, indeed, at anything in general. Often said of someone whose confidence exceeds his worth. Terry Duckworth 'fancies his chances with anything in skirts'.
fause: variant of 'false'; cunning, not to be trusted. 'As fause as a barrowload of monkeys' is a common northern expression.
favour someone; favour something: resemble someone. Babies are generally said by admirers to 'favour' either their father or mother.
feel clever: feel well, healthy, as in, 'Our Jack had a late night, and he's not feeling too clever.'
feel rough: the opposite of feel clever. Also expressed as 'feel like something the cat dragged in'.
feet under the table: to have one's feet well under the table is to be 'well in with' someone; be familiar, cohabit with.
fellow-me-lad: the fellow about whom the speaker is talking. Similar to the Cockney expression, 'my son', but always directed at a younger person.
fent: fabric from the end of the roll, a remnant sold cheaply at market stalls for dressmaking.
fetch up: to raise a child. Hilda Ogden described her lodger Henry Wakefield as 'fetched up to be a good worker'. Those who lack the social graces, according to Hilda, 'are not fetched up, they're dragged up'. A quite different meaning is to wretch, vomit or be sick: 'He were fetching up over the rail on that boat trip.'
fettle: to repair, or improve the condition of; also, prepare. An old Lancashire expression used by Albert Tatlock and Stan Ogden. 'That engine sounds as though it needs fettlin'. A related expression is the familiar 'in fine fettle', describing a person in vibrant form.
(pull one's) finger out: signifies 'Get moving!' An admonition to improve performance, popularized by the Duke of Edinburgh's advice to British workers, 'Gentlemen, pull your fingers out.' The derivation, as Partridge diplomatically explains, is to 'stop scratching your backside and get on with the job'.
fist someone: to strike someone. Len Fairclough 'fisted' several people when pushed beyond endurance. In the general sense of 'to fight', the expression is more than 680 years old.

'Flaming Nora!'

fixed: situated. 'How are you fixed?' means 'can you arrange or manage' something. For example, 'How are you fixed to lend me a fiver, our Terry?' or, 'How are you fixed for a night out?'
Flaming Nora!: 'Flipping 'eck!'; or as Americans put it, 'Holy cow!' Nora is the Dark Lady of *Coronation Street* vernacular. The expression has been used by countless characters, from Elsie Tanner to Jack Duckworth, yet veteran Street scriptwriter H.V. Kershaw admits, 'I have used this phrase many times without any knowledge of the lady'. Even the peerless scholars of Oxford University Press dictionaries can provide no clue to Nora's history.
flannel: smooth talk, superficial attempt to appease; or salesman's patter. Partridge gives the related 'flannel-mouth' – an old Canadianism for 'a well-spoken person'.
flash Harry: a 'greasy' character of extravagant habits, someone who is common, vulgar, but self-assured, gangster-like. From 'flash', meaning 'loud' and in poor taste.
flatspin: overworked, anguished, desperate to the point of panic. 'The vicar walked in and there was washing everywhere. I was in a right flatspin.' From aeroplane terminology – 'go into a flatspin'.
flies' cemetery: slang term for **Eccles cake**, due to the number of currants in it.
flipping: used, like 'flaming', 'frigging', 'bleeding' etc., without any particular meaning, to strengthen an oath or exclamation. As in, 'flippin 'eck'.
flit: *do a flit* – leave, *do a bunk*. Also, to move house. The Websters 'flitted' to Southampton.
fluffing: a seldom-heard adjective, or adverb, used as a substitute for 'flipping' or 'flaming'. As in, 'Who cares about the fluffin' football scores'.
flummoxed: somewhere between flustered and puzzled. Mavis Riley spends her life in a permanent flummox.
flutter: an adventure or gamble. Jack Duckworth to Hilda Ogden after mutual

success at betting on the horses: 'Let's have another flutter, shall we?' – which is slightly naughty, because it also connotes lovemaking. Partridge derives the word from 'the flutter of excitement'.

Mavis is **flummoxed**.

flyer: *do a flyer* is to vanish overnight without settling one's debts or rent; one can also 'do a **bunk'** or 'do a runner'.
footer, footie: diminutive for football.
footling: trivial, insignificant. Alf Roberts once became 'sick and tired' of filling 'footling little barmcake orders'. From 'footle', to trifle, which may come from futile.
for a gold clock: for anything, for any amount of money. 'I wouldn't have his job for a gold clock.'

'Here we go! Here we go! Here we go!'

fratchy: quarrelsome, irritable. Ena Sharples and Annie Walker used the expression when discussing others: 'What's up with her – she's fratchy this morning.' From *fratch*, quarrel or make an unpleasant or creaking noise.
fry-up: in its simplest form, fried food. A fry-up, considered a dream dish by Street folk for whom cholesterol holds no fears, can be the great British breakfast of bacon, egg, sausage and fried bread, or, then again, it can be cold leftovers re-heated. Mashed potato, cabbage, etc. are often fried up (the burned, crispy pan-scrape is considered a great delicacy) and topped with a fried egg. As Hilda says with a chuckle: 'Wrap yourself round that, chuck. It'll put hairs on your chest.'
full monty: everything included. To avoid the awkwardness of stumbling through an unfamiliar menu, someone might tell the waiter: 'We'll have the full monty.'
full of running: in top running condition, as of a car.
fussed: excited, upset. Mavis is frequently fussed when the Kabin paper-boy fails to turn up.
fussock (also *fuzzock)***:** an idle woman with no inclination for domestic duties. The male equivalent is **wuzzock**. Hilda uses the expression, confident that she could never be accused of the same thing herself.

gadding: going out for pleasure or entertainment. 'Where's Audrey gadding off to now?' Often, 'gadding about'. The O.E.D. puts little credence in an origin having to do with gadflies and suggests *gadling*, a vagabond.
gaffer: the boss, as in, 'Hey up – the gaffer's coming', a usage dating from at least the seventeenth century. Can also denote an old man – 'An old gaffer was sitting on a fence, so we asked him the way'. Possibly from a telescoping of 'grandfather'.
game of soldiers: see **beggar this for a game of soldiers**.
gannet: originally sailor's slang for a greedy seaman, after the bird; now of greedy persons generally.
ganzie: a jersey or pullover, from a dialectical variant of 'guernsey'.
gather someone: to understand someone, as in, 'Come again, I don't gather you' or 'Could you please repeat that, I don't get what you're saying'. Simply an extension of the common verb *to gather,* meaning to comprehend.
gawp: gape at, ogle, gawk at. The noun, *a gawp*, means a fool, as in, 'That lad you brought home looks a right gawp, Sue.'
gee-gee: racehorse. From children's slang, 'gee' being the shortened form of 'Gee up!' The perhaps punningly-named barmen Fred Gee spent many hours picking gee-gees from the newspaper.
gerraway: get on with you! An expression of friendly disbelief. 'Give over!' has the same meaning. Also 'Ger on with you!' or 'Gerraway with your bother!'
get at someone: deliberately annoy someone, nag.
get done: to be arrested or punished. 'I see Mrs so-and-so's been done for shop-lifting.' More generally, to suffer injury or abuse.
get in: to *get someone or something in* – to summon someone, obtain or purchase something. Also *get 'em in* – to order drinks in a pub (see **shout**).
get kalied (pronounced 'kale-eyed')**:** to get very drunk indeed. 'Kay' is a prefix implying affliction, as in 'kay-handed' for left-handed, or 'kay-legged' meaning bow-legged.
get knotted: 'Go to hell!' 'Stuff it!'.
get landed: become burdened with something. As Curly might say to Terry when arranging dates: 'A foursome's alright for you, mate, but I'll get landed with her sister.'
get off!: 'Knock it off!', 'Stop it!', 'Give over!'.
get on: to fare, manage, as in, 'How did young Sue get on at her interview?' 'Get on!' or 'Get on with you!' implies disbelief.
get on one's wick: get on one's nerves: 'Percy really gets on my wick.' The expression, oddly enough, comes from 'Hampton Wick', an area of London, which became rhyming slang for 'prick'.

get shut of: get rid of. Also, 'want shut of' – 'You want shut of that Duckworth lad. He's bad news.' See **shift.**
get stuck in: 'Get cracking!'. Urges involvement, especially in eating or working.
get the push: to be dismissed, especially from a job. Analogous to the North American 'be shown the door'. Also *get the chop.*
get the run of: understand how something is done or works; by extension, understand how to take advantage of someone: 'And he just sits there while you do the washing and cooking – he's got the run of you.'
get your skates on: 'Get going!' 'Hurry up!' See **on your bike**.

'Get your skates on!'

ginnel: variant of gennel, a narrow alleyway between buildings. When a particularly observant viewer pointed out that the gentlemen's lavatory in the Rovers appeared to open into Albert Tatlock's kitchen, next door, changes were made when the new *Coronation Street* set was built. A ginnel was constructed between the pub and No.1 so that there could be no further confusion. The O.E.D. records usages in this sense from 1669.
girl's blouse: describes an adult male who has a low pain threshold, a 'sissy'. When trying to remove a splinter someone might say: 'Hold still you big girl's blouse. It won't hurt.'
give a good name: generally speak well of. As in, 'The Duckworths? Nobody gives them a good name.'
give it a rest!: 'Give over!', 'Pack it in', 'Knock it off' etc.
give it up!: See previous entry.
give one's best leg: to give anything, as in, 'I'd give me best leg for a week in Benidorm just now.' 'I'd give me back teeth. . .' may also be used.
give over!: expresses either disbelief, in the sense of 'Come off it!', or an appeal to stop. When Vera nags Jack, he pleads: 'Give over, Vera!'
give someone the air: dismiss someone, tell someone to 'get lost'.
glam up: make glamorous. Bet Lynch always gets 'glammed up' for a night out. Fashion note: Bet has worn 513 different pairs of earrings since she first appeared on *Coronation Street.*
go a bomb: or *go down a bomb,* go over really well, 'with a bang'. Rita Fairclough's nightclub act used to 'go down a bomb' with the audience.

'**Give over**! They don't look like a pair of knickers to me.'

go in for: enter, undertake or apply for. One can 'go in for' a competition or a career.
go it a bit: overdo something, or exaggerate – 'Hey, that's going it a bit, i'n't it?'
go on: see **get on,** and over page.

'**Glam**? Well, to be frank Gail, it looks like Minnie Caldwell's cat to me.'

Rita **goes down a bomb**.

go on at: nag, scold, deride. Before Jack Duckworth took his window-cleaning round, Vera was always 'going on at him' to get a job.
go spare: to go wild with anger, 'go crazy'.
gob: mouth. Sometimes prefaced by 'big'; dates from at least Shakespeare's day.
gobslotch: glutton. Used by Ena Sharples to express distaste at someone's eating habits. See previous entry.
gobsmacked: taken aback as though hit in the mouth (see **gob**). Also, to have assumed a hurt and puzzled expression. Mavis Riley looks permanently gobsmacked.
gold clock: see **for a gold clock.**
good nick: common Britishism for good condition.

Hilda looks **gobsmacked**.

good on ya!: 'Good for you!'
good 'un: a kind or commendable person. 'She's a good 'un, is our Hilda.' See also **have a good 'un**.
gooseberry: to be the odd one out in a trio, particularly when the other two are in love. From *gooseberry* meaning chaperone or matchmaker.
gor blimey: sometimes 'cor blimey'. A euphemistic contraction of an ancient oath: 'God blind me if . . .' See **blimey o'reilly!**
Gordon Bennett!: an exclamation pronounced with great exactitude 'GORdon BENnet!' Possibly an allusion to wealthy American newspaperman James Gordon Bennett (1841-1918), whose engagement to wealthy Caroline May was dissolved after a well-publicized incident at her palatial home: Bennett shocked Washington society by arriving 'a bit kalied', and mistook the drawing-room fireplace for a urinal.
gormless: 'clueless', dim-witted. From 'gome', circa AD 1200, for 'to take heed', take notice. 'Gome' later became 'gaum'.
got it in one: got it (figured something out) on the first guess.
got up like a dog's dinner: see **dog's dinner.**
gradely: good, decent, of merit or worth. 'She's a gradely lass.'
graft: work, almost always prefaced by 'hard'. Also used as a verb, to work.
greedy guts: a greedy person, a **gobslotch**. Compare **misery guts.**
grumblebelly: an expression used by Hilda, in particular, to describe a discontented person.
gyp: to bother or cause annoyance. Jack Duckworth's stomach 'gives him a bit of gyp' after a night on the beer, a condition also described as 'gyppy tummy'. The O.E.D. gives the derivation as possibly 'Gee up!' – a rider's command to his horse, perhaps because when the horse complies the rider gets bounced around. See **collywobbles**.

'Yes, I'm sure it is **gradely** up here, Victor. I just thought we'd be happier living in a house.'

ha-bloody-ha: an example of tmesis, a linguistic construction in which a word is placed inside a different compound word. Sarcastic for 'I don't find that funny in the least'.
hab-dabs: usually, screaming hab-dabs. 'Heebie-jeebies', 'willies', 'screaming meemies'; in other words, an extreme state of nervousness or jumpiness. Also *hab-nabs*.
half a bitter, half a lager, etc.: half a pint of the specified libation.
half-inch: to steal; rhyming slang for 'pinch'.
hand-off: to give someone a hand-off is to give as good as one gets, to fend off. A rugby term meaning to push away a tackling opponent with the heel of the hand.
hand rag: someone whose hard work is taken for granted. See **skivvy**.
hand's turn: small service. Annie Walker would return home from an afternoon with the Lady Licensed Victuallers to find that barman Fred Gee 'hadn't done a hand's turn'.
hang about!: 'Hang on!' 'Be patient!' To hang about can also mean to loiter – 'hang around' in American vernacular.
hang for a sheep as a lamb: connotes that there is nothing more to lose by continuing a certain course of action. That is, one might as well be hanged for stealing a sheep as for stealing a lamb. If Jack knows that his tea is going cold while he is drinking in the Rovers, he might as well have another pint – and hang for a sheep as a lamb – as he is in trouble anyway.
hang one's cap up: to make oneself at home somewhere, to become familiar with. Also, to become engaged or settle down.
happen; happen that: maybe; it could be. 'Happen I'll get married when I'm good and ready.'
hard ched: sarcastic expression of sympathy. A variation of 'hard (cheddar) cheese'. Equivalent to the American 'tough toenails', or 'that's too bad'.
hard cheese: see previous entry.
hare off: run off at great speed, like a hare. 'Where are you haring off to, Hilda?' Also *hare around*, chase around, run all over.
harp: persist with a topic to the point of boredom. 'He's always harping on about having to work Saturday mornings.' Very common in U.S. and Canada.
have a go at: to attack verbally, to tear strips from. 'Don't go in, Brian. Ivy's really having a go at George.' Applied to enterprises, it of course means attempt, undertake.
have a good 'un: a salutation, wishing the hearer a good day, celebration, holiday, etc.
have one yourself: when buying a drink at the Rovers, one tips the barman and barmaid by offering to buy them a drink. 'Two pints of bitter and one for yourself,

Betty.' 'Ta love, I don't mind if I do.' The French *pourboire* gives the exact idea. Acceptance in liquid or negotiable tender is the server's choice.
have someone on: play a joke on someone, deceive or trick.
heck as like: 'No way!', or 'Indeed not!' 'You owe me a tenner.' 'Do I heck as like.'
hell as like: heck as like, only more so.
hey-lads-hey: uproar, free-for-all. 'As soon as someone thumped him it was hey-lads-hey.'
hey up!: a greeting or sign of recognition; 'Look who's here!' Alf Roberts' favourite expression. May also be used to alert listeners to events or trouble: 'Hey up! Here's Hilda on the warpath.'
hiddle: hide. An Alf Robertsism. 'Audrey, I'll hiddle that damn magazine if you don't put it down and listen.'

'Hey up!'

high jump: see **be for the high jump.**
hold up!: 'Wait a minute!' 'Hold on!', 'Hold your horses!'.
home: see **What's that when it's at home?**
home and dry: safe and sound.
hop it: take flight, disappear, 'beat it!' 'We'll mind your car for 10p, Mister.' 'Hop it, kid.'
hot pot: meat and potato stew, probably related to 'hotch-potch'. Known in Liverpool as 'scouse', from which the people of that city derive their nickname, Scousers. Annie Walker refused to introduce 'pub grub' to the Rovers because it was **common**, and prepared hot-pot instead.
how yer diddlin'?: 'How are you?' 'How's it going?'
hump: *to give or get the hump*—make or become disgruntled, out of sorts.
hungry work: an undertaking that consumes much energy, makes one hungry.
hush: silence, especially 'a bit of hush'. 'Let's have a bit of hush, please! Bet wants to say a few words.'
hutch up!: 'Move over!' 'Make some room!' 'Sit closer'. Comes from *hutch* via *hunch*, as in hunchback, meaning to squat or crouch. (A hutch is also a constraining little hut.) A D.H. Lawrence poem goes: 'Sleep-suave limbs of a youth with long, smooth thighs/ Hutched up for warmth. . .'

I ask you: 'Would you believe it?' 'Would you **credit** it?'
I don't think!: said to indicate irony or scepticism. Elsie, recalling the night of the Street gas leak, and the cold reception residents received from Ena when they were evacuated to the Glad Tidings Mission: 'She made us very welcome – I don't think!'
ill-getten: dishonestly obtained. From 'ill-gotten'.
in all my born puff: in all my born days. See **Nellie.**
in the chair: one is 'in the chair' if responsible for paying for a round of drinks. The pun, of course, is on formality – being the person in authority.
in the club: pregnant. The full form is 'in the pudding club', pudding being a euphemism for semen.
(be) in with a shout: succeed, make a breakthrough (worthy of a cry of victory).
it's a doddle: 'It's no problem'. Possibly from the carefree idea of 'dawdle'.
it's alright for some: indicates that others are more fortunate, or somehow better-off, than the speaker: 'Mike and Susan are honeymooning in the Caribbean.' 'Eee, it's alright for some!'
it's not on: 'No dice!' 'No way!' 'Nothing doing!'

jack it in: give up, throw in the towel.
jammy: lucky. A 'jammy beggar' is someone blessed with good fortune, a much-sought commodity in Coronation Street.
jar: a pint of ale, as in, 'Are you coming out for a jar tonight?'
jessie: a derisive term for a man who displays effeminate traits. 'A right jessie' is something akin to a big **girl's blouse**.

'I'll feel a right **jessie** carrying that, Mrs. Walker.'

Jigger (something): to hell with . . .
jiggered: exhausted, knackered. Coronation Street people are often jiggered after a day at work. 'I'll be jiggered!' is used when one is non-plussed.
jiggery-pokery: trickery, devious behaviour, hocus-pocus. From the Old Scottish *'joukery-pawkery'* (O.E.D.).
job: thing, as in, 'It's a good job you didn't light a match near that gas leak.' Also, task – 'a long job' is an enterprise which requires patience and commitment. As a foster mother, Rita Fairclough found it a 'long job' winning the confidence of the thirteen-year-old she fostered.
joe soap: rhyming slang for 'dope' (a stupid person). Also a friendly fool; someone too willing to please, a 'mug'.
jumped up: arrogant without just cause, egocentric. Someone suffused with a sense of her own importance might be described as 'a jumped up little madam'.
just saying: see **only saying**.

kalied (pronounced 'kale-eyed'): drunk. See **get kalied.**
keen as mustard: sharp, avid, 'doesn't miss a trick'. A homely pun on Keen's Prepared Mustard. In their different ways, both Annie Walker and Bet Lynch were as keen as mustard with their bar staff. It is hard to 'pull one over' on someone who is as keen as mustard.
keep your hair on!: 'Be patient!' 'Calm yourself!' 'Don't fly off the handle!' The American equivalent is 'Keep your hat on!'

'**Keep your hair on**, Elsie, I'm just saying it doesn't look like a trouser suit.'

keg-legged: or *cork-legged* so drunk one can hardly walk; that is, legless, as kegs are rolled from place to place. 'Keggle', a northern expression no longer used, meant to stand unsteadily. Cork-legged gives the impression of the rolling gait of someone with an artificial limb.

kick into touch: reject, remove from consideration. A rugby term meaning to kick the ball out of the field of play. Someone may start a new venture only to abandon it, or kick it into touch. Also, to jilt someone – 'she kept dragging me to look in jewellers' windows, so I kicked her into touch.'
kickoff: *for a kickoff* – for a start. 'What have you got against our Terry?' 'Well, for a kickoff, he fancies his chances.'
kid: term of affection, especially favoured by Vera: 'Hiya, kid.' 'Our kid' is also one's brother or sister. In common use throughout the English-speaking world.
kip: now common in Britain for sleep. 'Stop mithering and let's get some kip.' Also a bed – 'in kip'. Partridge, says that *kippe* in Danish means 'brothel'.
kit out: supply all the necessaries for an occasion or undertaking. Jack Duckworth, when Vera was having a new frock made was heard to say, 'There's never been as much to-ing and fro-ing since they kitted out Princess Di for't Royal flippin' wedding.'
knacker: destroy, break; see next entry.
knackered: worn out, tired, physically exhausted. The knacker's yard is where old work horses are taken to be slaughtered. See **jiggered**.
knees up: a boisterous party, a 'rave', where guests are likely to get up and dance energetically. From the popular Edwardian party song, Knees Up Mother Brown.

A **knees up** in the **Snug**.

knock about with: to be friends with, to go out with. From *knock about* – to be footloose, 'bounce' from place to place.
knock back: take aback, **knock for six.** Also, reject, as in, 'I put an insurance claim in, but they knocked it back.'
knock cobs off: to win a (verbal or physical) fight.
knock for six: bowl over, devastate, 'knock one's breath out' (figuratively). From cricket.
knocker-up: A man employed in the heyday of the textile industry to knock on bedroom windows in the early morning with a long stick, to wake families for the first shift of the day. Old members of the Street used to reminisce in the Snug about the knocker-up.
knocking on: elderly, of a ripe old age. 'I don't know how old Percy is, but he's knocking on.'
know one is born: used in the negative, meaning to be free from everyday troubles. 'It's alright for him. He doesn't know he's born.' – he has an easy life.
know one is landed: as in, 'He doesn't know he's landed.' Expresses a similar idea to **know one is born.**
know one's onions: to have expert knowledge. 'I don't care what you say about Brian, he knows his onions when it comes to car repairs.'

landed: *be landed with* – be stuck with, burdened with, lumbered with, as in, 'It's all very well you going off with the boys. I'm landed here with the kids.' But compare **know one is landed.**

lardy cake: a heavy cake made of a sort of bread dough, very sticky and greasy. English food expert Elizabeth Davis says it should come with a health warning.

lark: business, especially when it is still a novelty. 'This pub lark's a pushover, Vera', Jack Duckworth has said. 'Lark' and 'caper' are seldom used by those who have been working at a particular business for some time. Compare **caper.**

lash out: spend extravagantly. In 1971, when Hilda won £500 on the Premium Bonds, she 'lashed out' on a drinks trolley. Compare **splash out.**

latch on: realize, become aware of. 'We were pulling his leg for a good ten minutes before he latched on.'

lather: pronounced, of course, with a flat 'a' sound. A state of excitement bordering on panic. Mavis was 'all of a lather' when a bird was stuck in her chimney; the common North American equivalent is 'in a lather'.

laughing: *be laughing* – have it made, succeed, be safe and secure, as in, 'If that gee-gee comes up in the 3.30, I'll be laughing.'

laughing boy: ironic description of a man who looks unhappy, or is grumpy: 'Hey up, here comes laughin' boy.'

leave it out!: 'Cut it out!' 'Leave it alone!'

legless: drunk to the point of being unable to stand. Usually said in exaggeration.

lemon: something or someone undesirable. An expression which can be used to describe oneself in an embarrassing situation: 'I felt a right lemon.'

Legless.

less of the: 'There's no need for', 'Let's not have', as in 'Less of the sarky tone, friend.'
let: to have landed or settled. 'I don't fancy that barm cake, Alf. A fly's just let on it.' From 'alight'.
let in for something: set oneself or others up for problems or difficulties.
let the dog see the rabbit: make way, make room, 'let me attend to it'.
let the grass grow: take things slowly or in their own time – usually in the negative. 'When you've got plans, you don't let the grass grow, do ya;' that is, don't let the grass grow *under your feet*.
let's be 'avin you: an appeal to Rovers' customers to drink-up at closing time. Former landlord Jack Walker used to say: 'Come on, let's be 'avin you. Have you got no homes to go to?' More generally, it is used to obtain service, attention, cooperation. See *sup up*.

'Ere! There's a fly just **let** on this butty.'

lie-in: the act of sleeping late. The dream of every *Coronation Street* early riser is to 'have a good lie-in'. See also **over-lie**.
listen on!: 'Pay attention!' 'Listen!'
loaf: rhyming slang for head, as in, 'use your loaf' (of bread).
lob-codded: lop-sided, cock-eyed, not perpendicular. See, **skew-whiff.**
look a treat: see **treat**.
lookout: concern, problem, 'business', as in, 'That's your lookout'. A look out, which is less common, means a 'stepping-out', a recreational stroll. Mavis Riley said she took her lunch at the Rovers because she 'fancied a look out'.
lot: a group of people or things, usually a motley or a mess — not complimentary.

'They're a right lot those Duckworths' or, 'Young Dennis was alright, he just got in with a bad lot.'
lug: to carry a heavy load. 'I've been lugging that shopping all over Weatherfield to find you a pair of shoes.' In daily use in North America.
lugs: ears, as in, 'Pin back yer lugs and listen to this.' Also known as 'lug-holes'. The North American equivalent is 'jug-handles'.
lumber: to be, or get in lumber is to end up in trouble. 'He's not in lumber again, is he?' Thought to be a cant corruption of Lombard Street Prison.
lumbered with: burdened with, **landed with**. From eighteenth-century slang meaning 'pawned', hence stuck with something that does not belong to one.
lummock: (also lummox) a big, ungainly or clumsy person. Hilda occasionally said to Stan: 'Get out of me way, you great lummock!' See **wuzzock**.

madam: a cheeky, 'hard-faced' girl or woman. 'A proper little madam', is the way Hilda usually uses the word.
maiden: wooden clothes horse.
make a bomb: make a large amount of money; 'explode' into financial success. Compare **go (down) a bomb**.
make a go: to *make a go* of something — to succeed at an undertaking or enterprise.

'I'll **swing for** that little **madam**! I told her I wanted a tint.'

make a good job of: do something well; or, ironically, really make a mess of things. 'You really made a good job of that', can be taken either way, depending on emphasis.
make a meal of: to overdo something; make a big deal of something that doesn't merit it.
make a packet: make a pleasing sum of money. Something can also *cost a packet* – be expensive. Spain's popular holiday coast, the Costa Brava, is now nicknamed the Costa Packet by the British.
make any odds: make any difference. As in, 'It don't make any odds whether you like it or not.'
make do with: to make the best of limited resources. 'You'll have to make do with a cold wash. The boiler's broken.' In everyday use in North America.
mam: children refer to their mother as 'our Mam'. Brian Tilsley and Terry Duckworth both call their mothers 'Mam'.
mangle: old-fashioned, manual clothes-wringer. In the early days of *Coronation Street* every self-respecting backyard had its mangle. A large hand-cranked wheel propelled two wooden rollers between which wet clothes were fed to squeeze out the water. 'Mam! Our Tommy's got his fingers caught in the mangle', was a common childhood drama.
manky: naughty or spoiled, as in, 'You manky devil!' Partridge suggests it derives from the French *manqué*, 'lacking' or 'flawed'.
mardy: spoiled, used to having one's own way. As a noun, 'a real mardy-pants'. From 'marred', in an adult, an indication of sulkiness or moodiness.
mark someone's card: verbally tackle someone, tell someone what's what in no uncertain terms. A betting term, from marking a race-card.
marker: *to have one's marker down* – to reserve something, claim first right to. When mechanic Kevin Webster's family moved to Southampton he 'had his marker down' for a flat above Alf Roberts' corner shop.
marmalize: to assault violently — thankfully, it is used mostly in exaggeration. See **spifflicate**.
marps: the children's game of marbles.
mash: to brew tea. 'I'll mash a pot of tea.'
maul: to handle or play roughly, as in 'Stop maulin' about, you lads.'
me and all: (also, her and all, them and all, etc.) me, too.
me laddo: fellow-me-lad. Often means 'my friend' or pal, but also the man about whom the speaker is talking.
me old darlin': sadly, this charming expression left *Coronation Street* with Len Fairclough when he died on the road, coming home from an extra-marital tryst. Usually said by one man of another to mean 'old buddy', 'old pal', 'me old cock'. John Mortimer's famous barrister, Rumpole of the Bailey, has been known to apply the phrase to judges and colleagues he especially loathes.
mee-maw: to gesticulate behind a person's back.
mess someone about: give someone a difficult time. See **no messing**.
midden: rubbish heap, dung heap. From the Scandinavian for muck-heap. When Alf Roberts sat on a Christmas pudding that Percy Sugden had cooked for charity, he decided to 'chuck it in't midden' so no one would be any wiser. Written usages since the fourteenth century.
middling: quite well, in moderate health. 'How are you keeping?' 'Middlin, thanks.'
miserable article: see **article**.
misery-guts: a chronically and obviously depressed person, or someone who

constantly grumbles. Compare **greedy-guts**.

missus: more commonly known as 'the wife'. Jack, in his more affectionate moments, refers to Vera as 'the missus'.

mither: nag, bother, worry, harass; as in, 'Stop mitherin, will ya?' From the seventeenth-century *moider*, or *moither*, which also meant 'to talk incoherently or foolishly. . . to wander or ramble in one's mind'. The word is still pronounced 'moither' in some parts of the north of England. Weatherfield, as part of Manchester, prefers the harder sound. Mithered mothers are often plagued by **mardy** children.

mockers: *to put the mockers (muckers) on something* – to jinx, curse or ruin. From 'muck', as in, 'to muck something up'. 'Muck up' was a printers' substitute for a now common vulgarism that rhymes with it.

moggy: either a cat or a mouse.

monkey run: also known as 'the monkey walk'. A place, or part of a street, where teenagers ritually parade up and down in gangs, trying to attract the opposite sex. Almost redundant in the age of discos, but older Street residents often recall it. The term was imported from London.

moon-flet: moonlight-flit, disappear without notice to avoid rent.

mope: to sit lethargically and feel sorry for oneself. Mavis sometimes mopes about past love affairs. In everyday use in North America.

more's the pity: 'So much the worse'.

moth-eaten: exhausted, unable to cope or concentrate because of someone's behaviour. 'Oh shut up, Terry! You've got me moth-eaten.'

muck: dirt. Occasionally surfaces in expressions such as 'where there's muck there's brass (money)' or 'as common as muck'.

muck about: play around, refuse to take seriously.

mucker: best mate, pal. From army slang, 'to muck in', to share food, lodging, etc.; or to help someone in some task. For 'put the muckers on', see **mockers.**

muck in: see previous entry.

mug: fool, fall-guy. Sometimes lengthened to 'muggins' in reference to oneself: 'Who'll carry the can if it all goes wrong? Muggins here.' Possibly from the all-purpose mug, into which anything can be poured.

murder: as in, 'I could murder a cuppa'. Expresses an overpowering need for.

muriel: Hilda Ogden's pronunciation of 'mural'. She has a blow-up of an Alpine scene on her wall. Many viewers have written to ask where they could buy one.

mushy peas: a popular accompaniment to fish and chips. Split green peas in an almost *puréed* (mush) state. Served at Jackson's chippy and yet another reason for the fame of British cuisine.

mutton dressed as lamb: someone trying to ape the style of those above his – or more particularly her – social station. A tasteless dresser who may also be described as 'all top show' or 'all fur coat and no knickers'; **common**, as Hilda would call them.

my son: East End London (Jewish) version of **me laddo**. Mike Baldwin and Terry Duckworth use it often.

naff all: nothing, a phrase of probably obscene origin. Terry Duckworth, looking down the jobs column of the *Weatherfield Gazette* in search of a job for his father, remarked that there was 'naff all in it'. 'Naff orf!' popularized by Princess Anne, in an unguarded moment, is of obscure origin.
nana (sometimes pronounced *nar'na*): someone who is soft – like a banana – in the head. Often 'right nana', or 'great nana'.
nark: a state of annoyance; *to be narky*, or to be 'in a right nark' is to be very upset.
narrow squeak: a near miss, a near calamity.
natter: a chat. Also known as a 'chinwag'. A natter over a cuppa is a time-consuming Street occupation.
navvy's hanky: *to have a mind like a navvy's hanky* – to have lewd thoughts, a mind as dirty as a labourer's handkerchief. Intellectually, one can also be 'as thick as a navvy's bootlace'.
need one's head feeling: 'need to have one's head examined', in the sense of phrenology – the art of reading 'bumps' on the skull — rather than psychiatry.
Nellie: *'Not on your Nellie*!' The long form, now obsolete, is 'Not on your Nellie Duff!' – rhyming slang for 'not on your puff', meaning 'not on your life'.
Newton & Ridley: brewers and purveyors of beer to *Coronation Street*, and owners of the Rovers Return. Until the Great Fire, 41,100 pints had passed over the bar to appreciative customers.
nick: long-established cant for jail; *to nick* means to steal. Something can also be 'in good nick' – in good condition, of merchantable or serviceable quality.
nicker: one pound sterling, a 'quid'. As in, 'Twenty-five nicker, right down the drain.'
niggled: annoyed, vexed, pestered. From 'niggling' – petty, picayune.
nineteen to the dozen: see **talk ten to the dozen**.
nippy: lively, sharp. Waitresses in Lyons Corner Houses, famous British eating establishments of the inter-war years, were called 'nippies'.
no danger!: for sure, without any doubt. 'You cross me, mate and I'll swing for you, no danger!'
no messing: without delay, without fuss; for sure, 'no danger!'
no mistake!: used for emphasis to mean 'you'd better believe it!' or 'that's the Gospel truth!' 'You lay one finger on our Terry and you'll have me to deal with, and no mistake!'
nobbut: nothing but. 'He's nobbut a lad.'
noddle: brains, or head. As in, 'Use your noddle!' As a verb, gape at, ogle.
noggin: a social drink, a tête-a-tête. 'I'll see you in the Rovers for a quick noggin.'
nosey parker: someone with an unhealthy interest in other people's business. Vera, for instance, is 'pretty nosey' while Hilda, of course, is 'dead nosey'.

not half: said ironically to mean 'completely'. Kevin Webster once had his eye on a girl who was 'not half tasty'.
not on: usually preceded by 'it's', meaning 'No dice', 'No way'.
not on your Nellie: see **Nellie.**
not so dusty: reply to a greeting or comment on one's well-being, meaning 'not too bad'. Equivalent to **middling**.
not to worry: 'Don't worry about it'. 'Things will be alright'.
nous (pronounced nowse): common sense, instinctive intelligence, awareness, initiative. 'He hasn't got a lot of nous for a lad of twenty, has he?' From the Greek philosphical term!
nowt: nothing. 'We've nowt in for tea.' 'I owe nowt to nobody', Albert Tatlock would say, asserting his independence. See **summat**.
nowty: in a child, naughty, badly behaved; in an adult, cross or ill-tempered. Phyllis knows that Percy is 'a nowty beggar', but likes him too much to let it bother her.
nutter: person given to unpredictable behaviour; nut, **barmpot.**

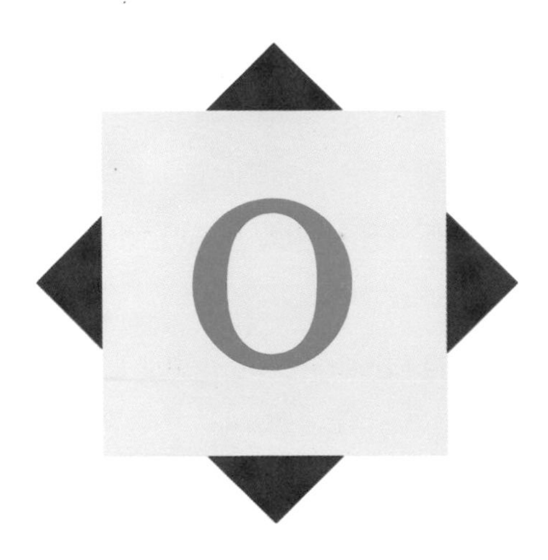

oar: *stick (put) one's oar in* – interfere, provoke trouble. Percy Sugden is always 'sticking his oar in where it's not wanted'.
odds: *What's the odds* – 'what's the difference'. Also, *it doesn't make any odds,* – 'it makes no difference'. Jack, having that extra pint in the Rovers when he knows he is late for dinner: 'Well, what's the odds – I may as well be hung for a sheep as a lamb.'
off one's own bat: on one's own authority. Jack Duckworth, for instance, knew that the brewery had chosen him as the Rovers' barman – 'not Bet Lynch off her own bat'. From cricket.
off one's trolley: **barmy,** off the rails, crazy.
off-colour: *to look, or be, off-colour* – look ill, not oneself. 'Eee, luv, you look a bit off colour.' 'Peaky', meaning pale, is also used in this context.
oi!: not the Yiddish cry of despair, but an Anglicized version of 'hey you!' Compare the more jocular, **Hey up**!, meaning 'Look who's here'. In genuine usages, there is always the merest whisper of an 'h', a very slight aspiration, at the beginning of the word.
old Bill: the police. The source is an old soldier depicted in wartime cartoons (1914-1918), noted for his sour disposition.
olleys: the children's game of marbles. See **marps**.
(the) old feller: one's father.
on about: talking about, often in usages that indicate confusion or annoyance. 'What are you on about with this Christmas pudding caper?' 'What are you talking about with this Christmas pudding business?'
on the fiddle: on the take; literally 'playing around' with finances.
on the quiet: on the sly, surreptitiously. 'She's supposed to be engaged, but she's been seeing that other bloke on the quiet.'
on the slate: on credit, on tick.
on tick: on credit. From an abbreviation for 'ticket'. Florrie Lindley, who bought the corner shop from Elsie Lappin in Episode One, asked: 'What 'appens if they ask me for tick?' See **slate**.
On your bike; on your skates: 'Get going!' 'Beat it!' In the sense of 'hurry, or you'll be late', this expression was made notorious by British employment minister Norman Tebbitt who urged the unemployed to 'get on their bikes' to search for work.
one for yourself: see **have one yourself**.
one-off: a one-time only event.
only saying: usually said in self-defence when someone takes umbrage at a remark; as in, 'Is it any business of yours what I spend my money on?' 'Well, I was only saying. . .'
(the) other: sex. Despite early language constraints on *Coronation Street*, 'the other' has crept in at least once. Bet, discussing a holiday with Rita, remarked:

'Sorry luv, no **tick**.'—Florrie in the corner shop.

'There'll be plenty of the other'. 'What's the other?' Mavis asked, typically befuddled. 'Sex', whispered Rita.

other half: that is, 'the other half' of a pint of beer. 'I'll have the other half now, Betty, luv.' The expression has nothing to do with any bizarre system of ordering or selling drinks, but is simply a subtle way of conveying familiarity.

our: like 'your', frequently used to indicate a family relationship, or other intimacy. 'Our Andrea', for example, is a term of great affection compared with 'their Terry', which has a vastly different emphasis, bordering on contempt. 'Our kid' is one's sister or brother.

over the brush: usually to 'live over the brush'—cohabit without being legally married. The original expression was evidently 'over the broomstick', from makeshift marriages performed by couples jumping over a broomstick. Dicky and Audrey Fleming, two teenage runaways masquerading as man and wife, were the Street's first couple to live 'over the brush'. Since then, there have been remarkably few. Even Elsie Tanner, whose love affairs were legion, always maintained a threshold of respectability.

over the odds: more than one expects to pay; over the difference or cost. 'Here's a tenner. If that's over the odds, just make sure you come back with the change.'

over the top: too much, overdone: 'Calling me mean is a bit over the top, I'm just frugal.'

over-lie: to sleep in by accident; as opposed to a lie-in, which is intentional.

owt: anything. See **summat**.

oy!: see **oi!**

pace eggers: Albert Tatlock's expression for local mummers or morris dancers. From an ancient custom called pace-egging – rolling decorated eggs down a hillside at Easter-time.
pack up something: to give something up, **jack it in.** 'I'm going to pack up smoking when I've finished this packet.' Or, 'I've had it with studying, Dad. I'm going to pack up school.' Also, *pack something (or someone) in*.
painted: what one is popularly made out to be. As in, 'She's not so bad as she's painted.' Vera, however, invariably is.
parkin: a cake made from oatmeal and molasses (or syrup), traditionally eaten on November 5, Bonfire Night. Ena Sharples' parkin, made to an old recipe, was the best in the street.
parky: cold, chilly. 'It was parky up that ladder this morning, Hilda.' 'Aye, Stanley. Well we've all got us cross to bear.'
parlour: front room used only for special occasions. At one time also common in North America. See **come through**.
past it: no longer capable of performing a particular function; over the hill. Stan Ogden, after years of illicit visits to the mysterious lady at No.19 Inkerman Street, finally admitted that he was 'past it'.
peaky: see **off-colour.**
peg: or peggy – child's tooth. 'Has Nicky got any of his peggies yet?'
penn'th: literally, penny's worth, full value. Usually 'two penn'th', as when someone watches their chips being served in Jackson's chippy and remarks, 'Hey, put a few more on, cock! I want me full two penn'th's worth.'
pie: along with chips, one of the most popular main-course items of food in the Street. One of the loveliest lines came from an old character who said: 'I were so hungry, I had that pie inside me before steam hit ceiling.'
pie-can: fool. Usually used in mild sarcasm or humorous banter. 'Daft pie-can' adds insult to injury. Of obscure origin.
piecer: Ena Sharples used to relate how she started her working life as a piecer in Hargreaves Mill. The job involved fastening, or 'piecing', together yarn-ends on a spinning mule frame.
pig in muck: used to describe someone who is really in his element: 'as happy as a pig in muck'.
pig-in-the-middle: someone caught in the middle of a disagreement or unpleasantness. Betty Turpin found herself pig-in-the-middle when the brewery appointed her temporary manager of the Rovers Return in place of Bet Lynch. From a children's game in which two throw a ball to each other, while the third stands in the middle trying to intercept it.
pinny: pinafore, apron. Hilda is rarely seen without one. Since the series started 26

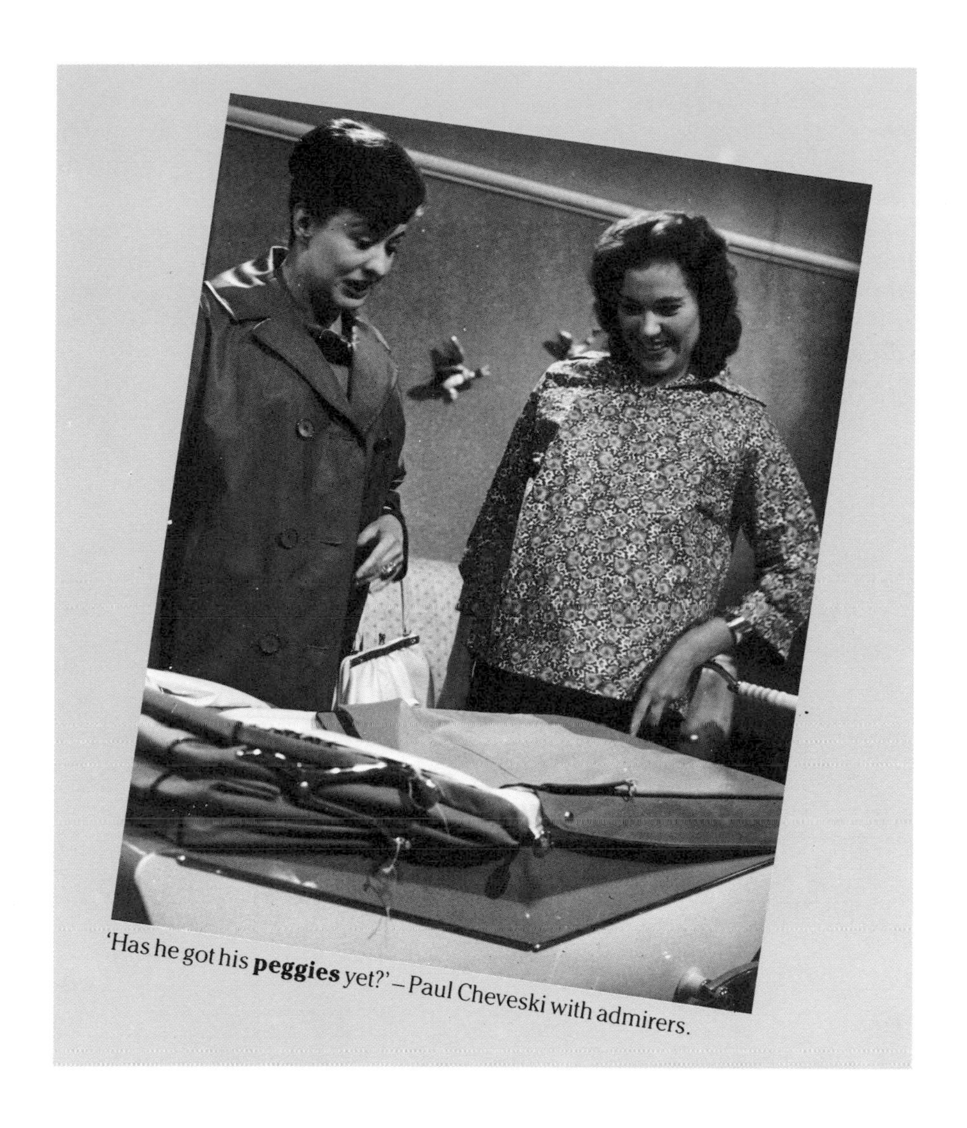
'Has he got his **peggies** yet?' – Paul Cheveski with admirers.

years ago, she has worn out five pinnies, four head-scarves and four sets of curlers. The Street wardrobe department has to scour market stalls for Hilda's pinnies, which are extremely hard to find because the style is so dated.
pip: nerves; as in, 'you get on her pip'; from the mid-eighteenth century, meaning to be depressed or take offence.
play silly beggars: fool around, connive, scheme. 'Silly buggers' is an old card game, while 'silver beggar', in underworld cant, was someone who lodged false claims for compensation.
play the devil with: bedevil, or cause trouble to.
play merry hell with: see previous entry.
play thump with someone: play the devil with, albeit the implication here is more violent. 'If I find out who broke that window, I'll play thump with them.' The suggestion is, of course, that the offenders will be beaten.
plonk: cheap wine, or sometimes, wine in general; perhaps ironic, from the French *blanc (vin blanc:* white wine). Partridge suggests 'plink-plonk,' apparently the sound of wine being poured into glasses; others suggest an origin in the sound of cork being extracted from a wine bottle. Annie Walker once valiantly tried to introduce a 'cocktail hour' at the Rovers with a small selection of wines, but Hilda described it as 'like having tea in a dog kennel'.

pobs: pieces of bread soaked in warm milk; also porridge. Given to small children, invalids, and a greyhound, 'Fred's Folly', once jointly owned by Street residents. Pobs sustained the dog through the winter.
pole: *up the pole* – exasperated, angry or distraught, as in, 'Those kids have driven me up the pole today.'
ponce up: dress up, or 'doll up'. Although a ponce is a pimp, 'ponce up' is not necessarily derogatory between friends: 'Now Alf, where are you off to, all ponced up?' 'All done up like a dog's dinner', conveys the same meaning.
pong: offensive smell.

'What's that **pong**, Stanley?'

pooh-pooh: to pour scorn on something; to cynically reject. 'I told Mike Baldwin we'd work better with longer tea-breaks. But he just pooh-poohed the idea.' Common in North America.
pools: organized betting on the outcome of soccer games. The pools, or 'the coupon' as some call it, are seen as an opportunity to **make a packet** from just a few pence outlay each week.
poorly: ill. The reigning Miss Weatherfield claimed to be 'poorly' the day Alf Roberts booked her to officiate at the grand opening of the renovated corner shop. One can also *go down poorly* – become ill. 'Poorly' was popularized by northern comedian Reg Dixon, whose catchphrase was 'I'm proper poorly'. The only effective remedy for anyone who has 'come over poorly' is a good lie down and a nice cup of tea.
pop one's clogs: die.

pot-boiler: an on-going argument or point of contention.
pot-man: an under-barman who collects and washes empty beer glasses. From 'pot', a heavy beer mug or drinking glass.
potty: crazy, **barmy**; usually said in an amicable way.
pound to a pinch: *'I'll bet you a pound to a pinch. . .'* – I'll bet you something against nothing. A more common expression, 'a pound to a penny', illustrates the meaning more clearly. A 'pinch' originally was probably a pinch of snuff.
previous: *to be previous* – be premature, to put the cart before the horse. 'I'll need the money up front.' 'That's a bit previous. You haven't even done the job yet.'
prezzie: present, gift; another in the long catalogue of British colloquial diminutives, along with 'Crimbo' for Christmas and 'this affie' for this afternoon.
prom: promenade or walkway. Blackpool Prom, otherwise known as the Golden Mile, is the mecca of undiscerning holidaymakers, and a favourite haunt of Bet and Rita. A cheap Stetson, emblazoned with the legend 'Kiss Me Quick', and a stick of candy floss are *de rigeur* when strolling on Blackpool Prom.
proper dinner: a substantial hot meal — usually meat and two veg, as opposed to, say, beans on toast. 'You need a proper dinner inside you in this weather, chuck.'
puddled: erratic, confused as if drunk; **barmy**.

'But Mr. Barlow, you told us this would be a **proper dinner**.'

pull a bird: acquire female companionship, even if only for the evening. Kevin is quietly proficient at pulling birds. Terry thinks he is, while Curly prefers a 'meeting of minds'.
pull a pint: draw a draught of beer, originally through traditional beer pumps, into a glass.
pull a stroke: pull a fast one, put one over, outsmart.

pull one's own wishbone: Custom has had it that a wishbone determined which of those pulling it apart would marry soonest. When Phyllis Pearce discovered that Emily Bishop had invited her heart-throb Percy Sugden for Christmas dinner, she wished 'Emily Bishop would pull her own wishbone' — find her own man to chase.
pull the other one: more fully, 'pull the other one, it's got bells on it'. An expression of disbelief implying, 'Do you take me for a fool?' The bells probably refer to those on a fool's, or jester's hose, attached at the knees.
pull someone up: correct someone forcefully, tell someone off.
punter: common British slang for 'Joe Public', or everyman, the average consumer. In underworld slang 'mug punters' are those foolish enough to work for a living.
push: the moment when action or decision cannot be avoided. As in, 'When it comes to the push I'll put in a good word for you.' See also **get the push**.
push off: generally, leave, depart – 'I'll have to push off now, Gail.' Also, as a command: 'Push off, pal!' — 'Go to hell!' 'Get knotted!'
push the boat out: treat oneself and/or others at unusual expense. Really blow the budget. Bet, at the end of a love affair, will 'push the boat out' to take her mind off things.
pushed: under pressure, late, bothered by many pressing obligations.
put a bed up: make up a bed with sheets and blankets.
put a sock in it!: 'Be quiet!' 'Belt up!'
put in the club: to make pregnant. The full form is 'put in the pudding club'. Equivalent to 'having a bun in the oven'. See **in the club**.
put one's coat on: leave. 'Don't worry, I won't be putting my coat on just yet.'
put oneself about: play the field, be one who likes a good time without serious romantic commitments.
put paid to: end once and for all. Percy would dearly like to 'put paid to Phyllis's nonsense', that is, bring an end to her unwelcome romantic overtures.
put the boot in: to add insult to injury; also 'take decisive action' (Phythian). Also, literally, to kick someone.
put the wind up: frighten, make someone nervous. To *get the wind up* is to experience the same emotions oneself.

quality folk: gentlefolk, professional people. Quality folk are the middle classes, typified by Dr and Mrs Lowther (Hilda used to **do** for them) and Kevin Webster's former girlfriend, Michelle Robinson, who came from the 'better' part of Weatherfield. 'Quality folk' would look on Street folk individually as either 'very reliable' or 'those awful people'.

Annie Walker — one of the Street's **quality folk**.

queer the pitch: ruin one's plans or prospects. From 'pitch' as in sales pitch, or performance in a show, not pitch as in soccer field. Worried about how local redevelopment would affect his garage, Brian Tilsley remarked that he hoped urban renewal would not 'queer his pitch'.

quicksticks: a short period of time — 'I'll be there in quicksticks'.

'You're **quids in** here, Bet. "Executive seeks sophisticated blonde with sense of fun . . ."'

quids in: 'We'll be quids in', Jack Duckworth said, trying to talk ex-Rovers barman Fred Gee into a shady business deal. Signifies one is doing well, or making a good profit – quids, of course, being pounds sterling.
quits: *to be quits* — to be even; to have evened the balance, monetarily or otherwise, in the sense of tit-for-tat.

rabbitting on: chattering incessantly.
rag: *to get one's rag out* – to get angry and fulminate. Also, *lose one's rag.*
rag bag: dishevelled or scruffy person.
rained off: of sporting or other out-door events, postponed or cancelled because of rain. North Americans say 'rained out'.
ram jam: full to capacity. 'I was lucky to get on that bus. It were ram-jam packed.'
rates: local taxes. 'On the rates' – on the taxpayer. 'It's all right for you Alf, wining and dining on the rates.' In 1975, Ernest Bishop formed W.A.R.P. – Weatherfield Association of Ratepayers – to protest against local rate rises.
rave-up: a party, a good time, knees-up. Sometimes shortened to 'rave'.
razzle: *on the razzle* – having a glamorous, extravagant outing. Bet Lynch is 'chuffed to little mint balls' when she 'gets dolled up to go on the razzle'.

Ken, Elsie, Albert and Annie **on the razzle.**

readies: ready cash, as in, 'I'd pay me rent, but I'm a bit short of the readies.' Or, as Mike Baldwin puts it: 'Sure we can do a deal, me old mate. But it'll have to be in readies.'
rec: recreational centre (playing field, park, etc.) See **Red Rec**.
recklin': the youngest in the family, an expression still used by the older folk on the Street.
Red Rec: Weatherfield's red-asphalted recreation ground, which gives rise to the expression 'as draughty as Red Rec'.
removals: services for transporting furniture and personal property.
right: real, veritable, as in, 'He's a right so-and-so.' Or, 'I'm a right muggins, me, for listening to you.' *Right* is also used to mean 'OK', 'well' etc., more or less meaninglessly, to make transition in conversation.
right one; right 'un: a real character, a real roustabout or rogue. Not quite a 'bad lot', but a rough diamond nonetheless.
rights: to have, or to put, or to see, to rights is to do the absolute proper thing. 'Rights' is in the legal sense of absolute propriety. Compare **bang to rights**.
ripstitch: one who is untidy, reckless or, in the case of children, literally prone to tearing clothes.
road: used as synonymous with 'way', as in, 'Keep out of me road.' 'Anyroad', in conversation, means 'anyway'.
roll on: used in the sense of 'hurry up', as when Betty Turpin says 'Roll on closing time!'
room to swing a cat: enough space to move freely in. Literally, space enough to swing a cat in a circle by its tail. 'There's not enough room to swing a cat in those new council flats.'
rough: *a bit of rough* – an uncouth, unmannered man, or a loose woman.
round: *bread, milk, window or newspaper round* – route tended by one who delivers any of these commodities, or cleans windows. After Stan Ogden died, Jack Duckworth bought his window round.
ructions: uproar, trouble. Said to derive from 'insurrection', but 'eruption' may be nearer the mark. 'There'll be ructions when Emily finds out they had a party while she was away.'
rum: a 'rum 'un' is a rascal or someone odd or unusual; a *rum do* is an odd or unpleasant state of affairs.
runner: *do a runner* – disappear, run off, do a bunk, **scarper.**
runt: derogatory term, used by Len Fairclough, of a weakling or diminutive person of unpleasant character. In everyday use in North America.

sack: *to sack someone; to get the sack* – dismiss, or fire someone; to be fired. From a practice of handing a workman a sack to gather together his tools before leaving.
safe as houses: very safe, secure, as if locked away.
same to you with knobs on!: identical to 'The same to you with bells on.' Reply to an insult or mockery: 'May you suffer a similar fate, only worse.'
sarky: sarcastic. 'Now don't be sarky!'
sarny: a sandwich. See **butty.**
say fair: be just, truthful, fair, absolutely precise: 'He may be broke, but he's a gent, and you can't say fairer than that.'
scarper: to do a **bunk**, run away. Possibly from the Italian *scappere*, to escape. Folk etymology gives *Scapa Flow*, the British Naval base where German vessels were *scuppered* after World War I. The expression was at one time stage slang for missing a theatrical engagement.
scoff: to eat very quickly, or voraciously. The word originated in South Africa, and the North American equivalent is *scarf*. 'Scoff' is also slang for food.
scorrick: a scrap or fragment. 'Did you see him scoff that? There's not a scorrick left.'
scrag: to assault, or rough someone up; figuratively, to ring someone's neck. Scrag was originally cant to describe hanging by the neck or garotting. Later it became sports slang for a neck tackle. *Scrag end*, or neck-end of beef is a popular Street dish.
scran: bread, food, sundry eatables.
scrat: to scratch. 'If you've got an itch, scrat it.'
screaming hab-dabs: See **hab-dabs**.
screwmatics: a jocular distortion of 'rheumatism', used in all seriousness by Hilda Ogden. This, and other near-misses, are fairly common among Weatherfield women of a certain age. Compare 'high potential' for hypertension; 'very coarse veins' for 'varicose veins' etc.
scrog: a fragment; like **scorrick**.
scrubber: girl of cheap tastes and low-life values; the analogy is to animals that inhabit scrub.
scruff: a scruffy, untidy person. Possibly from 'scruff of the neck,' used when despatching dogs and disreputable people. *Scruffy*: down at heel, unkempt.
scullery: the term for an old-style Street kitchen, with a slopstone sink, before houses were modernized.
see someone off: tell someone off, deal forcefully with someone, the implication being to see them off the premises.
see to rights: do the absolute proper thing. See **bang to rights**.
select: *the select* – see **snug**. 'Select' can also mean well-to-do, or respectable. 'Weatherfield isn't all scruffy, you know. There's some very select parts, too.'

send someone to Coventry: ostracize, give someone the silent treatment. The Street's most recent victim of this practice was Hilda's lodger, Henry Wakefield (see **blackleg**). There are many theories on the origin of the expression, among them, that Coventry was a Parliamentary stronghold where Royalist prisoners were kept during the English Civil War, or that Coventry townspeople were oppressively pious. It is also said that soldiers dreaded postings to Coventry because the townspeople resented their presence and ostracized women who consorted with the troops.
set one's cap at: have amorous intentions toward; Partridge dates it from the eighteenth century. Applied to women only.
settle someone's house: teach someone a lesson, give someone 'what for', as in, 'I'll settle his house for him.' Probably from *to settle someone's hash*, to defeat or kill – recorded as early as 1807 in the U.S., 1825 in Britain.
set-to: an argument.
shaker: a shocker, something that *knocks one for six*. Emily Bishop had a shaker when she discovered her second husband was a bigamist. See **facer**.
shape: behave in an efficient manner, pull oneself together. 'Come on, shape thissel!' In American: 'Shape up!'

Happy days — before Emily had a **shaker** about her husband.

sharpish: this very minute, immediately, as in the universal 'ten o'clock sharp'. 'They'd better show up sharpish, or we'll leave without them.' Compare with **smartish**.
shift: move, as in 'Shift yourself!' *Shift for oneself* — to manage without help or companionship. *Get shift of* – get rid of.
shirty Gertie: someone who is 'uptight' and looks down the nose at others (is shirty).
shop!: comparable to saying 'Anyone here?' when entering an apparently

unattended store.

shout: a noun signifying the act of paying for a round of drinks. 'It's your shout.' From the act of calling to the barman or barmaid. To *give someone a shout* means to consult or call on someone. See also **in with a shout.**

shout the odds: from racetrack slang, meaning to argue loudly, or protest indignantly.

show someone up: publicly embarrass or make someone look bad. Often said to children: 'Wait till I get you home. You'd show anybody up, you would.'

shufty: a look, as in, 'Have a quick shufty at this contract and see if you're agreed.' Partridge says military men picked it up in the Arab world and used it in such expressions as *shufti bint*, a ready and willing Moslem woman; a *bint* could be a girlfriend and/or a slut. A *shuftiscope* was military slang for sundry optical instruments, such as a telescope, periscope, even proctoscope.

shurrup!: 'Shut up!'

shut: see **get shut of.**

sick as a parrot: most put out, thwarted, extremely disappointed, ill. Street folk have been 'sick as a parrot' on several occasions when they won the football pools, only to find that the dividend was just a few pence. A cliché overworked by football commentators to the point of ridicule, along with 'over the moon' which means ecstatic.

'I feel as **sick as a parrot**, Dennis. Four draws up and I forgot to post the coupon.'

(to) side: put something to one side, tidy up, as in 'side the pots'.
simnel cake: traditional fruit cake made by Ena Sharples and Minnie Caldwell for mid-Lent Sunday.
since Adam were a lad: for a very long time. An expression often used by the late Jack Walker: 'Hilda Ogden's had that old sofa since Adam were a lad.' Jack Duckworth told firemen that the electrical wiring in the Rovers had been there 'since Adam were a lad'.
sken: a look at, squint at – 'let's have a sken'. From at least the early 1600s.
skew-whiff: askew, lop-sided. See **lob-codded.**
skidaddle: to run away, clear off hurriedly. 'There's a bobby coming – let's skidaddle.' Common in North America.
skinful: a surfeit, especially of drink, as in 'I had a skinful last night'. 'I've had a skinful of that bother'.
skint: flat-broke; from 'skinned'.
skive: *skive off* – shirk responsibility or disappear when duty calls. Partridge suggests it may originate in Lincolnshire slang for turning up the whites of the eye, as one may do at an unpleasant task. Compare **hop it.**
skivvy: act as a female servant or char. Also, someone who is overworked, or put upon, in some menial position. 'He treats her just like a skivvy at home.'
skrike: cry, complain, shriek, one who does this being a 'skriker'.

'Don't **skrike**, Minnie. It's only Stan taking up hang-gliding.'

skylark: to fool around, play, joke, trick. The O.E.D. awards the invention of the word to sailors, and quotes Falconer's *New Universal Dictionary of the Marine*: '*Skylarking*, a term used by seamen to denote wanton play about the rigging and tops or in any part of the ship.'
slag someone off: to verbally besmirch someone; possibly from the dialectical Scottish for 'to smear or spit on'.
slanging match: an argy-bargy in which the verbal mud is really slung (with the intention of making as much stick as possible).
slap: make-up, cosmetics. As Bet Lynch says: 'Get your slap on, and we'll go out on the razzle.' From theatrical slang, probably from the practice there of really slapping on make-up. 'Face' is an alternative expression: As she was driven away by ambulance from the Rovers fire, Bet, barely conscious, asked: 'Can you hang on while I put me face on.'
slap-up: superior, excellent, as in 'a slap-up **do**' – a really enjoyable party where expense is not spared.
slate: a record of accounts or other information, such as a criminal career: 'He's got housebreaking on his slate.' *On the slate*: on credit, **on tick**.
sling one's hook: (pronounced to rhyme with Luke) to disappear, **scarper,** do a bunk, **skive off.** Often applied to quitting a job abruptly or without warning.
slope off: leave quietly, sneak away.
slopstone: old-fashioned earthenware sink, now removed from all the houses in Coronation Street.

'Let's **sling our hook**, Vera. We'll never look like Joan Collins in these.'

slow coach: someone who 'dawdles': 'Come on, slowcoach. The Rovers closes in five minutes.' The North American equivalent is 'slow poke'.
slummock: someone who is dirty, untidy. Related to slovenly, lummocky. In an early Street episode, Albert Tatlock was told that people must think him 'a right slummock' to give him so many clothes for Christmas. Possibly the only occasion the expression was used on the series.
smartish: immediately, sharpish.
smile for the cat: (usually used in the negative): 'She doesn't have a smile for the cat' — she doesn't have a smile (kind word) for anybody. Usually said of someone who looks glum or depressed. Compare a **word for the cat**.
smoke: *The Smoke* London, since the turn of the century, before air-pollution legislation.
smudgy talk: dirty (smutty) talk.
snap: packed lunch, or other light meal, carried to work. Mining expression, but still commonly used in the Street. See **drinking**.
sneck: latch. 'Sneck the door' means fasten the door. See **unsneck**.
snitch: to inform on someone. Also known among children as 'to clat'. A 'clat-tale' is a tell-tale. Snitch in this sense is widely used in the U.S. and Canada.
snog: kiss, neck with. Possibly from 'snuggle'.
snug: *the snug* – a smaller room or parlour in a public house, so-called because it is cosier and more private than the main room. During the nineteenth century, snugs were thought undesirable because they provided an opportunity for crimes such as conspiracy, robbery, and prostitution. In the Rovers, the snug, with its single table and four chairs, was old Albert Tatlock's bailiwick — or at least he liked to think so.

Ena — Queen of the **Snug**.

sod: *'Sod off!'* 'Bugger off!' *Sod it, him, her, etc.* – to hell with . . . From an abbreviation of 'sodomite'. The fact that these expressions are blithely used on television attests to how little shock value they carry these days. The story goes, however, that the *Shorter Oxford English Dictionary* was once called the *Oxford Shorter Dictionary* to avoid the abbreviation S.O.D. Similarly, in *Under Milk Wood,* Dylan Thomas avoided censure, and censors, by reversing an entire word with his Welsh town of Llareggub.
soft: 'soft in the head', foolish. Also, by extension, someone who seems overly sentimental or kind. A 'soft touch' is someone from whom it is easy to extract money, or favours.
something like: an expression of approval: 'Now that's what I call something like!' An improvement, better than the previous item heard, seen or discussed.
sough: occasionally 'suff', and dating from at least the mid-fifteenth century. A drain, either in the form of an open ditch, or domestic foul-water plumbing. If there is trouble with the **cludgy**, it could be that the sough is blocked.

Albert has trouble with his **sough**.

sozzled, sossled: drunk, tipsy, 'soaked'. Perhaps from 'saucel'd', although the O.E.D. gives the derivation as 'sozzly' – wet, sloppy.
spare: see **go spare**.
spare talent: someone attractive and apparently available. See **talent**.
spark out: to become exhausted, entirely extinguished. A favourite expression of Eddie Yeats and Stan Ogden after a day's work.
speak as one finds: One of Hilda Ogden's expressions is 'I speak as I find',

meaning 'I don't mince words!' Or, as North Americans say: 'I call 'em as I see 'em', or 'I call a spade a spade'.
spifflicate: to defeat or completely ruin, to crush the life out of. Bet Lynch has applied it to her love-life. The origin is obscure, although, in the vein of **'marmalize'**, it could be an amalgamation of 'smother' and 'suffocate'. An American equivalent may be the fanciful 'murderate', popularized in 'Popeye' cartoons as 'moiderate': 'I'll moiderate ya, ya big lug!'
splash out: spend ostentatiously or beyond one's apparent means. Probably from 'make a splash', as the public effect is most important. Most Street families make a splash when their children get married.
spliced: married.

Fred and Eunice get **spliced**.

spot on: when Bet Lynch's books were audited, she was proud to say that they were 'spot on': exactly correct, **bang on**.
sprauncy: spry. 'You're looking very sprauncy today, Percy.'
squiffy: tipsy. Partridge says it probably derives from **skew-whiff.**
squiggy: *squiggy-eyed* – squinty-eyed.
stand by your beds!: 'Look sharp!' 'At the ready!' Obviously from military usage, hence Percy Sugden's affection for the phrase. Can also be said jokingly on the approach of an officious character, meaning 'Look out, here comes trouble'.
start as you mean to go on: advice customarily given to those about to embark on marriage, or other undertakings. It means, 'Stick to your guns, and don't let him or her boss you around'.
steady on!: 'Take it easy!' 'Hold your horses!' 'Steady!' is used in a jocular fashion between friends to mean 'Now, restrain yourself. Don't go over the top'.
steam radio: radio, 'steam' being a jocular way of emphasizing the technology of the pre-video era.
stick: punishment, abuse, 'what-for'. When a child is caned at school he is said to 'get the stick', but metaphorical uses are more common: for example, Mike Baldwin once said to a dinner companion, 'You gave that lobster a bit of stick, didn't you?' In the general sense of 'abuse' one can also, by linguistic magic, 'dish out some stick'. See also **up the stick**.
stick it: to persist at something, put up with, as in, 'This is the worst job I've had. I don't think I can stick it another day.' ('Stick it!' is also used in the American sense of 'Shove it!')
stick one on someone (or 'stick someone on'): a Len Fairclough practice: to strike someone a blow with the fist.
stingo: strong ale or beer.
stir it: stir matters up so as to cause trouble, or greater trouble; to be a stirrer. Hilda Ogden, a 'gifted' reader of tea leaves, cautions that to avoid doing this one should never stir another's tea.

Albert **started as he meant to go on**.

stitch up: to frame, swindle or out-manoeuvre. As a noun, *stitch-up,* a state of confusion or trouble deliberately caused.
Stone the crows: an exclamation of Australian origin, possibly derived from the fact that the bird is a farm nuisance. Then again, in ancient times, seeing a crow was an evil omen. The exclamation is a favourite of Mike Baldwin's. 'Stone the crows, Hilda! You'll be asking me for a rise next.'
stop in: to stay at home, as opposed to spending an evening out. 'Stop' on *Coronation Street* is generally used where North Americans, and the rest of Britain, would say 'stay'.
stop-out: *dirty stop-out* — addressed jovially to those who are not accustomed to staying out, but have arrived home late after a night on the town. Carries a teasing implication of naughtiness.
straight away: right away, immediately, straight off.
stranger things happen at sea: 'Anything is possible.' 'I can't believe Len was cheating on Rita.' 'Well, stranger things happen at sea.' See **worse things happen at sea**.
streaky bacon: a less expensive, fattier bacon, cut in strips (the fat and lean are in vertical strips) as compared to 'back' or 'Canadian' bacon. A popular line in Alf's Mini Market.
strength of it: *'That's the strength of it'.* 'That's the size of it'; describes something aptly, or fully, put.
strip: soccer or sports kit.
stroke: *to pull a stroke* – to pull a fast one; obtain an advantage by deception.
stroppy: obstreperous, touchy.
struck on: *to be struck on* – to be impressed by, or infatuated with. 'I'm not so struck on him' — 'I'm not exactly crazy about him'.
stuck: variant of 'schtuck' – trouble, difficulties often associated with lack of money. When Curly Watts quit his work as a bin-man and was left with no prospects, he remarked: 'I think we're in stuck' to which his friend and business partner Terry Duckworth replied: 'Dead stuck'. From German or Yiddish.

'I never knew Stan could **sup** so much.'

stuff: *bit of stuff* – see **bit of fluff**.
stumm: (pronounced 'shtum', with the u as in 'put') to be silent; from the German for dumb, mute, silent. Mike Baldwin frequently uses it as a command: 'Stumm!' One can also say, 'Don't worry mate, I'm stumm — my lips are sealed.'
sub: an advance, or loan (a subvention). Also, a verb: 'Can you sub me a quid till payday?'
summat: *summat and nowt* — something and nothing, meaning 'nothing to worry about'.
sup up: (each u is pronounced as in 'put') Jack Walker's exhortation to slow drinkers at closing time. Sup is a truly ancient word, from at least the ninth century when English was just developing; related to 'sip'.
suss out: discern, figure out.
swan in: a vivid phrase for gliding into a room or a gathering in a nonchalant, regal or pompous way. Annie Walker was highly proficient at swanning in. One can also 'swan off', which is usually associated with work, and meaning to wander off pursuing one's own interests.
swank: to show off, boast, act superior. In describing a schoolmate who had been engaged twice without seriously contemplating marriage, milkman's daughter Andrea Clayton observed: 'She just wants to swank about it.'
swing for someone: assail or assault someone. 'If he lays a finger on you, I'll swing for him.'
swing the lead: loaf around, avoid one's duty, **skive-off.** A corruption of *swing the leg,* itself originating metaphorically in a dog running on three legs, 'sometimes to rest the fourth, sometimes to elicit sympathy' (Partridge).
swish: something fashionable or fancy. One may attend a 'swish' function, otherwise known as a 'posh do'.
swiz: a cheat, swindler, fraud; from children's corruption of *swindle* via *swizzle*: 'He said he'd meet you there and didn't? What a rotten swiz!'
swot: to study hard, cram. Andrea Clayton was 'swotting for her A-levels'.

Annie, looking **swish**.

ta!: thanks; perhaps from baby-talk for thank-you.
tack: poor quality, tasteless food or beer; Eddie Yeats often used the word. From 'hard-tack' or dried meat.
take as meant: accept a remark in the spirit of goodwill with which it is offered, as in, 'I hope you'll take this as it's meant, luv, but that colour really doesn't suit you.'
take-away: a take-out restaurant.
take no notice: 'Ignore it', 'Never mind', 'Forget it'.
take the mickey: mock, be sarcastic, make fun of. Also referred to as 'taking the Michael', or even more laboriously, 'extracting the Michael'.
take someone off: imitate; mimic; 'do a take-off' (parody) of someone. The noun 'take-off' describes a mimic or an impersonator.
talent: attractive member of the opposite sex. **Spare talent** – one who is unattached.
talk broad: see **broad.**
talk ten to the dozen: see **ten to the dozen.**
talk wet: speak foolishly or without any evident knowledge of a subject; verbally play silly beggars.
tally: *living tally* – cohabiting; living together but not married. See **over the brush**.
tally-man: door-to-door money-lender or collector of credit payments. Elsie Tanner had many transactions with them.
tarrah!: a variant of the childish 'ta-ta', meaning goodbye.
tash: moustache; from a military slang abbreviation.
tat: rags, or more generally, junk, from a nineteenth-century colloquialism for rags or rag-gatherer, and the idea of something being in tatters. Tommy Deakin was the Street's 'tatter', or rag-and-bone man, who once stabled his donkey Dolores in the Ogdens' **backyard.**
tater: *to look, or be, a right tater* – look a real fool (literally, a potato-head). 'Tatered' once described the state of mind of soldiers despatched on fruitless missions; and a man was 'on for a tater' if infatuated with a barmaid.
tater 'ash: potato hash – a boiled meat and potato meal enjoyed by Stan and Hilda, and Percy Sugden.
tea up!: 'Tea is served!'
tearaway: a ruffian; a wayward, or violent person. Originally described a thief who specialized in purse-snatching.
teem: pour with rain. 'It's teeming down outside.'
tell tales out of school: gossip, speak of something one has no right or permission to speak of.
ten to the dozen: *to talk or prattle ten to the dozen* – to speak so fast that the listener might miss a few thoughts here and there. Another form, which takes the

mathematics in the opposite direction, is 'nineteen to the dozen'.
thick: stupid, dense, short for 'thick-headed'. A *thicky* is someone who is thick.
thick as two short planks: extremely dense, stupid, wooden-headed.
thingy: acceptable colloquial substitute for a name or person one is unable to recall. 'I bumped into Vera, Jack and their thingy on the market.'
think on: 'Take heed', 'Don't treat this lightly'. Also *think on it,* – an adjuration common in Shakespeare.
thirsty work: universal for work or other activity that makes one thirsty. Changing the barrels in the Rovers' cellar was 'thirsty work' as far as Jack Duckworth was concerned.
this affie: truncated version of 'this afternoon'. Compare **prom, wellies,** and **prezzie.**
thrash: a boisterous party, **knees-up,** bash.
thrutch: a very old, now dialectical word for push, thrust, squeeze. Ernest Bishop's brass band was once described as 'all thrutchin and pullin'.
tick: *in a tick*, or 'just a tick' — momentarily, as soon as possible: 'I'll be with you in a tick', Alf Roberts tells his customers, 'I'll be right with you.' From the ticking of a clock. See also **on tick**.
tiddly: tipsy. Tiddlywinks once described a disorderly public house or brothel.
tidge: a little bit, a mite. 'I'll just have a tidge more cake please, Emily.'
tin hat: *to put the tin hat on* – to do or say something objectionable that amounts to the 'clincher', or the 'last straw'. 'And when he made me pay my own bus fare home, that put the tin hat on it.' A variation is 'put the lid on it', a tin lid perhaps being a clue to the origin.
tip: garbage dump, refuse disposal centre. From the idea that garbage is tipped out of a truck. Used metaphorically to describe a house, or other premises, in a messy state. 'What a tip! It looked as though a bomb had hit it.'
tip someone the wink: caution someone, let someone in on a confidence. See **wink's as good as a nod**.
tip up: donate money to some end or cause, pitch in. 'Tip up while you've got some brass in your pocket.'
tod: to be on one's tod is to be alone, from the rhyming slang 'on your Tod Sloan' – on your own, Sloan having been a famous jockey.
toffee-nosed: stuck up, conceited — nose up in the air like a 'toff'. (A more appropriate spelling would be 'toffy-nosed'.) During the argy-bargy between the Duckworths and the Claytons, Vera called Connie Clayton a 'toffee-nosed cow'.
toff up: to dress elegantly or in an expensive manner, as a toff or dandy would. The male equivalent of being 'dolled up'.
to-ing and fro-ing: coming and going willy-nilly; 'running around' without apparent goal.
too right: said in hearty agreement: 'You'd better believe it!' 'You can say that again!' In American slang, 'Right on!'
top and bottom of it: the long and short of it.
touch: 'business', routine; implying falsehood on the part of the accused. 'Don't come that headache touch with me.' 'Don't try to pretend that you have a headache.' To touch someone up for money is to beg or con. See also **kick someone into touch**.
touchy: easily offended. In daily use in North America.
treat: special, especially nice; *do something up a treat* — do something in an especially delicious way. Of a person – *to look a treat.* A 'treat' is also a group outing, as in the annual Sunday school treat, or the pensioners' Christmas treat.

Brian, **toffed up** for his wedding day.

Stan and Hilda done up a **treat**.

'Well, he did **try it on**, Mrs. Sharples. But I told him I wasn't having any.'

try it on: attempt to get away with something, put one over. Also, to make amorous advances. 'He tried it on, but I wasn't having any.'
tumble: to figure something out, as in, 'Poor Percy finally tumbled that we were pulling his leg.' Perhaps from 'stumble upon'. Alternatives are 'it finally clicked', and 'the penny dropped', both mechanical allusions which suggest the tumblers of a lock clicking into place before a door can be swung open.
tuppence ha'penny: of little value, 'two-bit', as Americans say: 'She's a tuppence ha'penny snob.' Although Britain converted to decimal currency in 1971, the expression is still in use.
turmit: a Hilda Ogdenism for turnip, but see also *turmut* in the O.E.D. supplement. See **muriel**.
turn: dizzy spell, sudden change of emotion. 'She's had a funny turn. The doctor said it can go either way.'
turn up trumps: turn out successfully, surprisingly well. From playing card language for the highest suit.
twaddle: silly talk, banality, trivial nonsense. *Piffle* is an effective substitute.
twist someone: cheat someone, fail to deal fairly with. To 'drive someone round the twist' is to drive someone crazy or 'round the bend'.
twitchy: nervous, self-conscious.

unsneck: unfasten. As in, 'Unsneck the latch and let Eddie in.'
up the stick: or *up the spout* – pregnant, **in the club**. The origin is obscure but it may be obscene (stick=phallus), or simply from the idea of being in difficulties. 'Up the spout', can also mean haywire or defective — Terry Duckworth referred to the fuse-box which caused the Rovers fire as 'up the spout'. **Up the pole,** by comparison, means harassed or crazy: 'Percy drives me up the pole at times.'
up the pole: see previous entry and **pole**.
up to all sorts: that is, up to all sorts of naughty or roguish behaviour. See **all sorts**.
us: often used jocularly for me, my or our, as in, 'Give us a kiss!'

vinegar trip: a wasted or fruitless journey. 'I went on a vinegar trip to town – I forgot it were half-day closing.'

wacker: Liverpudlian, native of Liverpool. Eddie Yeats, Jed Stone and Len Fairclough were all wackers. The term originated from the practice of sharing food in poor parts of the city. (See **whack**.)
walk it: do something with consummate ease, the idea being that so little effort is needed, one can walk instead of run or ride. From racing jargon. Widely used.
walkabout: *go walkabout*—walk among others, from occasions when the Royal Family meets the public. Derives from pidgin English for journey. In factory jargon it may also mean to **skive,** or wander round the premises.
wally: a 'right wally' is a real jerk, a real nerd. Although *wally* in Cockney is a pickle, this usage may be an ironic twist on the Scots-English meaning, handsome, fine, admirable.
want: deserve, as in, 'he wants thrashing', or 'she wants telling'. Used to describe something, often unpleasant, that necessity or convention requires. Used in the sense of 'ought', as in, 'Somebody wants to punch him on the nose.' Also, *not want to know about something* – not want to have anything to do with something. When Ivy Tilsley told her son Brian that the Catholic Church forbade her to marry George Wardell because he was divorced – even though it was George's wife who had left *him* – Brian responded: 'If that's religion, I don't want to know about it.' *Not want to know someone* – to ignore someone or refuse to deal with someone, as in, 'I applied for a job but they heard I was a blackleg, and they don't want to know me.'
want shut of: see **get shut of**.
warm: *a warm* – the act of getting warmed up. As Jack Duckworth tells Alf Roberts on parky winter mornings: 'I'm not here to buy owt. I've just come in for a warm.'
watch on: to be on watch, or to mind something. When Alf was redecorating the flat above his shop, Audrey Potter, now Mrs Roberts, was watching on downstairs in the store.
wear something: tolerate something. 'He keeps snapping at me, and I just won't wear it any more.'
well in with: familiar with, a confidant or favourite of, what North Americans term 'on the inside track'. 'I'd watch her if I were you. She's well in with the boss.'
well out of: fortunate to be away from somewhere or something. To be better off left out of something. Mavis, for instance, was 'well out of marrying a wally like Victor Pendlebury.'
wellies: short for Wellingtons, waterproof rubber boots named for Arthur Wellesley, the Duke of Wellington. There is a story that Queen Victoria once asked the Duke what he called the boots he was wearing. When he said that one called them Wellingtons, Her Majesty remarked: 'Impossible. There could not be a *pair* of Wellingtons.' Wellies are notorious absorbers of perspiration. Jack Duckworth, savouring a pint of Newton & Ridley's, once waxed lyrically: 'Eee, it's grand stuff,

this. I could drink it out of Stan Ogden's wellie.'
welsh on: cheat someone, twist someone.
whack: or, *full whack* — a share, often monetary. As in, 'Oi! You didn't pay me the full whack.' *You can't whack it:* 'You can't beat it' (can't do better).
whacking: whopping, as in, 'a whacking great sum of money'.
what are ya'?: said to reinforce praise or criticism. In the phrase, 'You're a clever lad, what are ya?' it means, 'aren't you?' In the workplace, if one man makes a clumsy mistake, his partner may simply ask: 'What are you?' meaning, 'You idiot!'
what's that when it's at home?: or *What's he (she, etc.) when he's at home?* Signifies that the speaker has never heard of the entity or person under discussion – or is pretending not to, for dramatic effect. The implication is that only pedants, snobs, intellectuals or eccentrics would know better.

Stan the quiz-league contender: 'It was — er — what do you call it **when it's at home**?'

what's to do?: 'What's up?' 'What's going on?'
whimberries: bilberries, whortleberries. Customers in Jim's cafe occasionally ask for a slice of whimberry pie. *Whimberry* , first recorded in 1100, is the oldest of the three words for this blue-black wild fruit.
whip 'round: *to have a whip round* – to pass round the hat for someone, or to make a collection on someone's behalf. At the end of coach trips to Blackpool, Street residents always have a whip 'round for the driver.
whistle for it: an indication that remuneration will not be forthcoming, or that one will have to do without. 'So he wants his ten quid, does he? Well he can go and whistle for it.' Probably from the phrase 'whistle in the wind', meaning to achieve nothing.
Wigan Pier: See (a) **face as long as Wigan Pier**.
will you be told?: said when someone will not take the speaker's word for something. 'Will you be told, Vera? I can't work, I've pulled me back.'
winge (rhymes with 'cringe'): to whine, or complain. Rita often tells Mavis: 'Oh, stop your winging, will you?' Australians popularized the phrase 'winging Poms',

meaning moaning Brits.
wink's as good as a nod: 'a wink's as good as a nod to a blind man/horse/donkey'. That is, there is no need to explain further, I understand fully.
wishbone: see **pull one's own wishbone**.
with it: as well, also; as in, 'She's a nice looker, and brainy with it.'
without so much as a by-your-leave: peremptorily, rudely; without saying hello, goodbye, please or thank you.
witter: to **winge** or annoy someone by talking nonsense.

'Will you be told, Hilda! You haven't stepped in anything.'

word: *to have a word* – to have, or desire to have, a private conversation. Ivy is heard to say, 'I'd like a word in the office, Mr Baldwin.'
word – have a word for the cat: usually in the negative — 'She didn't have a word for the cat', means she had nothing to say to anyone. Compare with **have a smile for the cat**.
work a ticket: to be absent from work through illness, real or imaginary. From a military phrase (the U.S. equivalent of 'to be 4-F'), meaning to be physically unfit and subject to discharge from service.

worry-guts: a chronic worrier. Compare with **misery-guts**.
worse things happen at sea: 'Cheer up, things could always be worse'. Hilda once pulled the plug on Stan's bath-tub of home-made beer, fearing it was against the law. Stan was devastated. 'Worse things happen at sea', she told him.
would you credit it?: see **credit it**.
wouldn't say no: a coy way of accepting, or asking for something. 'Well, I don't normally, Mrs Walker. But I wouldn't say no to a small dry sherry.'
wuzzock; wozzack: awkward fool. Akin to **lummock**. Hilda to Stan: 'Out of me way, you big wuzzock.' Compare **fussock.**
wrong 'uns: wrong ones; disreputable people, ruffians, a 'bad lot'.

'Oh well, I suppose **worse things happen at sea**.'

yammer for: long for, yearn for something or someone. 'We were yammering for a toilet on that charabanc.'
yobbo: or yob — thug, brute, delinquent. Possibly from *lob*, a bumpkin or lout. Brian Tilsley, after foiling a robbery: 'A couple of yobbos tried to come it, and it was me that got done for it.'
yonks: *for yonks* – forever, a very long time. As in, 'It were a lovely funeral, but the vicar went on for yonks.'
you wha'?: (pronounced 'Ewe Wah?') 'You what?' meaning 'You did what!' 'Come again', 'you're kidding'. An exclamation of disbelief or shock, not a plea of momentary deafness.
you're a long time dead: the Weatherfield version of *carpe diem* (which is the Epicurean motto 'Seize this day!'). The famous English version is 'Gather ye rosebuds while ye may!' Or, as Mike Baldwin says: 'Another drink, Mavis? Come on, you're a long time dead.'

. . . now you're talkin'